From our Kitchen to Yours

Best-Ever
Sheet Pan & Skillet
Recipes

Delicious and satisfying dishes
for every meal!

To cooks everywhere who want to create easy & delicious one-pan meals for their family & friends.

Gooseberry Patch
An imprint of Globe Pequot
246 Goose Lane
Guilford, CT 06437

www.gooseberrypatch.com
1 800 854 6673

Copyright 2019, Gooseberry Patch
978-1-62093-335-0

••••••••••••••••••••••

Do you have a tried & true recipe... tip, craft or memory that you'd like to see featured in a **Gooseberry Patch** cookbook? Visit our website at www.gooseberrypatch.com and follow the easy steps to submit your favorite family recipe.

Or send them to us at:
Gooseberry Patch
PO Box 812
Columbus, OH 43216-0812

Don't forget to include the number of servings your recipe makes, plus your name, address, phone number and email address. If we select your recipe, your name will appear right along with it... and you'll receive a FREE copy of the book!

CONTENTS

Sheet Pans and Skillets
Make Every Meal Easy
4

Sheet Pans and Skillets
Make Every Meal Easy

You may have looked at the sheet pans and skillets in your cupboard for years, but until now you may not have realized just how amazing they are! That sheet pan that you thought was only for dessert bars, can cook a pork chop dinner in no time. And the ho-hum skillet you have reserved for frying an egg can make an amazing pizza or a dessert. The best part of all is that these humble pans can save you so much time and energy when it comes to clean up!

What is a Sheet Pan?

The name "sheet pan" can be a bit confusing. A sheet pan has a rimmed edge all the way around and is a type of baking sheet. Most cooks use the terms interchangeably as we have in this book. Some folks call a cookie sheet a sheet pan, but a true cookie sheet is flat with only one rimmed edge. A jelly-roll pan is not usually as thick as a sheet pan. In baking terms, a regular size sheet pan is really meant for restaurants. Most home ovens can accommodate a "half sheet pan" which is the typical size used, thus the confusion.

The typical sheet pan for home use is a heavy-duty, thick, usually aluminum, pan measuring about 18x13 inches or sometimes 15x10 inches with a rim all the way around that is about an inch tall. A quarter sheet pan is usually about 13x9 inches or sometimes 11x7 inches, which is great for smaller recipes.

Sheet pans are a must in your kitchen...they are hard working, affordable, durable and easy to clean. They conduct heat quickly and because they have a low edge, they allow the heat to circulate well and come in contact with more surface area on the food. The pan is large enough to let you spread out the meat or veggies without crowding. You can also use your sheet pan to bake cookies and bars if you like. Use a piece of parchment paper under your baked items for even cooking.

All About Skillets

These rough-and-ready pans can be made from cast iron, stainless steel, copper and stainless steel, or combinations of metals that transfer heat well. Choose a skillet that is easy for you to handle and make sure you have at least one that can go into the oven as well as on the stove top.

Cast-iron skillets are known for their heat retention and even heating and they stay warm longer than other metal types. You can bake or roast in a cast iron skillet as well. Some skillets have a non-stick surface which comes in handy for many recipes.

So purchase a sheet pan or skillet (or dust off those pans in your cupboard) and bring them out for all kinds of cooking adventures. Now you can make the recipes you love in one simple pan knowing they will be delicious. Plus you won't have to spend hours of clean-up time when dinner is over!

Jo Ann's Garden Frittata

CHAPTER ONE

WAKE-UP Breakfasts & Hearty Breads

Glazed Pumpkin Scones, Page 30

Spinach & Tomato French Toast, Page 48

Eleanor Dionne, Beverly, MA

Apple & Walnut Scones

These scones are wonderful fresh from the oven with hot tea or coffee. They can also be reheated. Wrap in aluminum foil and place in a preheated 375-degree oven for 5 minutes, then fold back the foil and heat for 3 to 4 more minutes.

Makes 8 scones

2-1/4 c. all-purpose flour
1/2 c. sugar
2 t. baking powder
1/2 t. salt
1/2 c. butter
2 eggs, beaten
1/4 c. milk
2 t. vanilla extract
1 t. lemon zest
1 c. cooking apple, peeled, cored and chopped
1/2 c. chopped walnuts
1/4 c. light brown sugar, packed
1 t. cinnamon

In a large bowl, combine flour, sugar, baking powder and salt; mix well. Cut in butter with 2 knives until crumbly; set aside. In a small bowl, mix eggs, milk, vanilla and lemon zest. Stir into flour mixture; dough will be sticky. Stir in apple. Grease an 11-inch circle on a baking sheet. Place dough on baking sheet; pat into a 9-inch circle. In a small bowl, mix nuts, brown sugar and cinnamon; sprinkle over top. Cut dough into 8 wedges. Bake at 375 degrees for 30 to 35 minutes, until lightly golden.

Rita Morgan, Pueblo, CO

Herbed Cheese Focaccia

This savory bread is a favorite, scrumptious for snacking or to accompany a tossed salad.

Serves 12 to 14

13.8-oz. tube refrigerated pizza dough
1 onion, finely chopped
2 cloves garlic, minced
2 T. olive oil
1 t. dried basil
1 t. dried oregano
1/2 t. dried rosemary
1 c. shredded mozzarella cheese

Unroll dough on a greased baking sheet. Press with fingers to form indentations; set aside. Sauté onion and garlic in oil in a skillet; remove from heat. Stir in herbs; spread mixture evenly over dough. Sprinkle with cheese. Bake at 400 degrees for 10 to 15 minutes, until golden.

Herbed Cheese Focaccia

Angela Murphy, Tempe, AZ

Breakfast Burrito Roll-Ups

Finger food for breakfast! Use whatever veggies you like.

Serves one to 2

3 T. green pepper, chopped
1 t. olive oil
3 eggs, beaten
1 T. water
2 8-inch whole-wheat flour tortillas
1/2 to 3/4 c. shredded Mexican-
   blend cheese

In a skillet, sauté green pepper in oil until tender. Remove pepper from pan. Whisk together eggs and water; add to hot skillet. Cook until set; do not stir or scramble. Flip to cook the other side. Cut in half; place half of eggs on each tortilla. Top with pepper and cheese; roll up and slice. Serve immediately.

Staci Meyers, Montezuma, GA

Mile-High Buttermilk Biscuits

The secret? Use a sharp biscuit cutter and don't twist it when cutting out your biscuits...you'll be amazed how high they rise!

Makes about one dozen

2 c. all-purpose flour
1 T. baking powder
1 t. salt
1/2 c. shortening, chilled in freezer
2/3 to 3/4 c. buttermilk
1/4 c. butter, melted

Mix together flour, baking powder and salt. Cut in shortening until mixture has a crumbly texture. Stir in buttermilk until well mixed and dough leaves sides of bowl. Dough will be sticky. Knead dough 3 to 4 times on a lightly floured surface. Roll out to 1/2-inch thickness, about 2 to 4 passes with a rolling pin. Cut dough with a biscuit cutter, pressing straight down with cutter. Place biscuits on a parchment paper-lined baking sheet. Bake at 500 degrees for 8 to 10 minutes. Brush tops of warm biscuits with melted butter.

Mile-High Buttermilk Biscuits

Kate Parks, Kettering, OH

Quick & Gooey Cinnamon Roll-Ups

These are so perfect on a cool fall morning! My husband and children adore these and they are so quick & easy to put together at the last minute. They're wonderful served alongside a tall glass of chocolate milk for the little ones or a cup of hot tea or coffee for the grown-ups. My little secret...they're delicious topped with ice cream for dessert too!

Makes 8 servings, 2 roll-ups each

1 c. sugar
2 t. cinnamon, or to taste
1/2 c. butter, melted
16 marshmallows
2 8-oz. tubes refrigerated
    crescent rolls

Combine sugar and cinnamon in a shallow bowl; place melted butter in another shallow bowl. For each roll-up, coat a marshmallow in melted butter, then in cinnamon-sugar. Place marshmallow at the end of a crescent roll and roll up. Fold in ends; pinch seams to close. Dip again in melted butter and coat in cinnamon-sugar. Place roll-ups on a parchment paper-lined baking sheet. Bake at 350 degrees for 10 to 12 minutes, until crisp and golden.

Tonya Sheppard, Galveston, TX

Huevos Rancheros to Go-Go

Serve these eggs with sliced fresh avocado for a deliciously different breakfast.

Makes 4 servings

2 c. red or green tomatillo salsa
4 eggs
4 8-inch corn tortillas
1-1/2 c. shredded Monterey Jack
    cheese or crumbled queso fresco

Lightly grease a cast-iron skillet; place over medium heat. Pour salsa into skillet; bring to a simmer. With a spoon, make 4 wells in salsa. Crack an egg into each well, taking care not to break the yolks. Reduce heat to low; cover and poach eggs for 3 minutes. Remove skillet from heat and top with eggs. Transfer each egg and a scoop of salsa to a tortilla; roll up. Sprinkle with cheese.

Huevos Rancheros to Go-Go

Sharon Velenosi, Stanton, CA

Whole-Wheat Soda Bread

This is a wonderful hearty, coarse-textured bread that's terrific with soups and stews.

Serves 4

1 c. all-purpose flour
1 t. baking powder
1 t. baking soda
1/2 t. salt
2 T. sugar
2 c. whole-wheat flour
1-1/2 c. buttermilk
1 T. butter, melted

In a large bowl, combine all-purpose flour, baking powder, baking soda, salt and sugar. Add whole-wheat flour; mix well. Add buttermilk; stir just until moistened. Turn dough onto a floured surface. Knead gently for about 2 minutes, until well mixed and dough is smooth. Form dough into a ball; pat into a circle and place in a lightly greased cast-iron skillet. With a floured knife, mark dough into 4 wedges by cutting halfway through to the bottom. Transfer skillet to oven. Bake, uncovered, at 375 degrees for 30 to 40 minutes, until loaf sounds hollow when tapped. Brush with butter; cool on a wire rack.

Vickie, Gooseberry Patch

Black Bean Breakfast Bowls

We love to serve this dish for breakfast on weekends. It looks so special...and tastes so yummy!

Serves 2

2 T. olive oil
4 eggs, beaten
15-1/2 oz. can black beans, drained and rinsed
1 avocado, peeled, pitted and sliced
1/4 c. shredded Cheddar cheese
1/4 c. favorite salsa
salt and pepper to taste

Heat oil in a skillet over medium heat. Add eggs and scramble as desired, 3 to 5 minutes; remove from heat. Place beans in a microwave-safe bowl. Microwave on high until warm, one to 2 minutes. To serve, divide into bowls; top each bowl with eggs, avocado, cheese and salsa. Season with salt and pepper.

Black Bean Breakfast Bowls

Jill Ross, Pickerington, OH

Breezy Brunch Skillet

Try this all-in-one breakfast on your next camp-out! Just set the skillet on a grate over hot coals.

Serves 4 to 6

6 slices bacon, diced
6 c. frozen diced potatoes
3/4 c. green pepper, chopped
1/2 c. onion, chopped
1 t. salt
1/4 t. pepper
4 to 6 eggs
1/2 c. shredded Cheddar cheese

In a large cast-iron skillet over medium-high heat, cook bacon until crisp. Drain and set aside, reserving 2 tablespoons drippings in skillet. Add potatoes, green pepper, onion, salt and pepper to drippings. Cook and stir for 2 minutes. Cover and

cook for about 15 minutes, stirring occasionally, until potatoes are golden and tender. With a spoon, make 4 to 6 wells in potato mixture. Crack one egg into each well, taking care not to break the yolks. Cover and cook over low heat for 8 to 10 minutes, until eggs are completely set. Sprinkle with cheese and crumbled bacon.

Trisha Donley, Pinedale, WY

Cheese & Basil Scones

These scones are a big hit at ladies' luncheons and book club meetings.

Makes one dozen

2 c. all-purpose flour
1/4 c. shredded Parmesan or
    Romano cheese
2 t. baking powder
1 t. baking soda
2 T. fresh basil, chopped
1/4 t. pepper
2/3 c. buttermilk
3 T. olive oil
Optional: 1 egg, beaten

In a bowl, combine flour, cheese, baking powder, baking soda, basil and pepper. Add buttermilk and oil; stir just until moistened. Knead gently 3 times on a floured surface. Line baking sheet with parchment paper. On lined baking sheet, pat dough into a rectangle; cut into 12 squares. Pull apart slightly. If desired, brush dough with egg to glaze. Bake at 450 degrees for 10 to 12 minutes, until golden. Serve warm or at room temperature.

Cheese & Basil Scones

Amy Butcher, Columbus, GA

Pesto & Green Onion Omelet

Preserve the fresh herb flavors of summer...make your own pesto sauce to fill this yummy omelet. It's easy!

Makes 3 servings

2 t. canola oil
4 whole eggs
4 egg whites
1/8 t. salt
1/8 t. pepper
2 T. water
1/4 c. green onions, chopped
1 T. favorite pesto sauce
Garnish: green onion tops, cherry
    tomatoes, fresh parsley

Add oil to a skillet over medium heat, coating sides and bottom well. Combine eggs and egg whites. Beat until frothy. Stir in salt, pepper, water and onions. Add mixture to hot skillet, and cook without stirring, lifting edges to allow uncooked egg to flow underneath. When almost set, spoon pesto sauce on half of omelet. Fold other half over, slide onto a plate and garnish with green onion tops, tomatoes and parsley. Cut into 3 sections.

Connie Hilty, Pearland, TX

Breakfast Pizza

Is there anything better than pizza for breakfast? You are going to love this recipe!

Serves 2 to 4

11-oz. tube refrigerated thin-crust
    pizza dough
14-oz. can pizza sauce
16-oz. container ricotta cheese
1/4 c. fresh oregano, chopped
favorite pizza toppings
4 eggs
salt and pepper to taste

Roll out dough into a 13-inch by 9-inch rectangle; transfer to a greased rimmed baking sheet. Spread pizza sauce on dough, leaving a 1/2-inch border. Top with cheese, oregano and other pizza toppings. Bake at 500 degrees for 4 to 5 minutes, or until crust begins to turn golden. Crack each egg into a small bowl and slip onto pizza, being careful not to break the yolks. Bake for another 5 minutes, until eggs are done as desired.

Breakfast Pizza

Diana Chaney, Olathe, KS

Cinnamon French Toast Dippers

Little hands love to pick up these crisp golden French toast sticks! Spoon a dollop of the sauce into a cup and top with toast sticks for an easy-to-handle breakfast.

Serves 2 to 4

4 eggs, beaten
1/2 c. vanilla Greek yogurt
1/4 t. cinnamon
4 thick slices day-old bread,
    each cut into 3 to 4 sticks
1 to 2 T. butter, divided

In a shallow bowl, whisk together eggs, yogurt and cinnamon until blended. Soak bread sticks in egg mixture, turning once. Melt one tablespoon butter in a skillet over medium heat. Working in batches as needed, add bread sticks to skillet. Cook until golden on both sides. Add remaining butter as needed. Serve French toast sticks with Maple Dipping Sauce.

Maple Dipping Sauce:
3/4 c. vanilla Greek yogurt
1/4 c. maple pancake syrup
1/8 t. cinnamon

Combine all ingredients; stir well.

Dobie Hill, Lubbock, TX

Buttermilk Cinnamon Rolls

These no-yeast rolls are super easy and fast to make and are always a treat!

Serves 15

3 c. all-purpose flour
4 t. baking powder
1/4 t. baking soda
1 t. salt
1/2 c. cold butter
1-1/2 c. buttermilk
1/4 c. butter, softened
1/2 c. sugar
1 t. cinnamon

In a large bowl, combine flour, baking powder, baking soda and salt; cut in cold butter until crumbs form. Stir in buttermilk until well blended; knead dough on a lightly floured surface for 4 to 5 minutes. Roll out to 1/4-inch thickness; spread softened butter over dough to edges. In a small bowl, mix sugar and cinnamon; sprinkle over dough. Roll up jelly-roll style; cut into 1/2-inch slices. Place on 2 greased baking sheets; bake at 400 degrees for 10 to 12 minutes.

Buttermilk Cinnamon Rolls

Virginia Watson, Scranton, PA

Grandma's Warm Breakfast Fruit

Keep this delectable fruit compote warm and ready for brunch in a mini slow cooker.

Serves 6 to 8

3 apples, peeled, cored and thickly
    sliced
1 orange, peeled and sectioned
3/4 c. raisins
1/2 c. dried plums, chopped
3 c. plus 3 T. water, divided
1/2 c. sugar
1/2 t. cinnamon
2 T. cornstarch
Garnish: favorite granola

Combine fruit and 3 cups water in a cast-iron skillet over medium heat. Bring to a boil; reduce heat and simmer for 10 minutes. Stir in sugar and cinnamon. In a small bowl, mix together cornstarch and remaining water; stir into fruit mixture. Bring to a boil, stirring constantly; cook and stir for 2 minutes. Spoon into bowls; top with granola to serve.

Kelly Gray, Weston, WV

Christmas Eggs

I used the eggs-in-a-hole idea for this recipe. My boys know it's Christmas when I start serving these eggs! They're so pretty on a plate at Christmastime, but fun to eat year 'round too. If you're not a fan of grits, you could serve them over buttered whole-grain toast.

Makes 6 servings

1 red pepper, sliced into 6, 1/4-inch
    thick rings
6 eggs
salt and pepper to taste
cooked grits
Garnish: chopped fresh parsley

Spray a large sauté pan or skillet generously with non-stick vegetable spray. Add red pepper rings and cook over medium-high heat, about 5 minutes on each side. Crack an egg into each pepper ring. Reduce heat to low. Cook to desired doneness, about 5 to 6 minutes. Season with salt and pepper. Use a spatula to remove eggs from pan and place one egg over a serving of grits in each bowl. Sprinkle with parsley.

Christmas Eggs

Gail Blain Prather, Hastings, NE

Nutty Skillet Granola

Fill small bags with this easy-to-fix granola...perfect for grab & go breakfasts and snacks.

Makes about 7 cups

1 c. quick-cooking oats, uncooked
1 c. old-fashioned oats, uncooked
1 c. sliced almonds
1/2 c. chopped walnuts
1/2 c. chopped pecans
1/2 c. wheat germ
1/4 c. oil
1/2 c. maple syrup
3/4 c. light brown sugar, packed
1 c. raisins

In a large bowl, mix oats, nuts and wheat germ; set aside. In a large cast-iron skillet over medium heat, combine oil, maple syrup and brown sugar. Cook, stirring constantly, until brown sugar melts and mixture just begins to bubble, about 3 minutes. Add oat mixture; stir well to coat completely. Reduce heat to medium-low. Cook, stirring occasionally, until mixture begins to sizzle and toast, about 3 to 4 minutes; be careful not to burn. Remove from heat; stir in raisins. Cool for 10 minutes; transfer to an airtight container. Will keep for up to 2 weeks.

Joshua Logan, Corpus Christi, TX

Egg & Bacon Quesadillas

So quick and so yummy...they will ask for more.

Serves 4

2 T. butter, divided
4 8-inch flour tortillas
5 eggs, beaten
1/2 c. milk
2 8-oz. pkgs. shredded Cheddar
   cheese
6 to 8 slices bacon, crisply cooked
   and crumbled
Optional: salsa, sour cream

Lightly spread about 1/4 teaspoon butter on one side of each tortilla; set aside. In a bowl, beat eggs and milk until combined. Pour egg mixture into a hot, lightly greased skillet; cook and stir over medium heat until done. Remove scrambled eggs to a dish and keep warm. Melt remaining butter in the skillet and add a tortilla, buttered-side down. Layer with 1/4 of the cheese, 1/2 of the eggs and 1/2 of the bacon. Top with 1/4 of the cheese and a tortilla, buttered-side up. Cook one to 2 minutes on each side, until golden. Repeat with remaining ingredients. Cut each into 4 wedges and serve with salsa and sour cream, if desired.

Egg & Bacon Quesadillas

Kathrine Moore, Kalso, BC

Kathy's Denver Sandwich

This is our idea of a good breakfast sandwich! Try it with diced ham too.

Makes 3 servings

4 slices bacon, chopped
1 T. onion, chopped
2 T. green pepper, chopped
3 eggs, beaten
1/4 c. shredded Cheddar cheese
6 slices bread, toasted and buttered

In a cast-iron skillet over medium-high heat, cook bacon until partially done but not crisp. Add onion and green pepper; cook until softened. Add eggs and cook to desired doneness. Sprinkle with cheese; cover and let stand until melted. Cut egg mixture into 3 pieces; serve each between 2 slices of toast.

Jo Ann, Gooseberry Patch

Jo Ann's Garden Frittata

Family & friends are sure to love this savory egg dish. It's filled with brightly colored vegetables...beautiful to look at and delicious to eat.

Makes 8 servings

4 thick slices bacon, chopped
1 onion, diced
1 red pepper, thinly sliced
1 c. corn
1 c. green beans, thinly sliced
1 bunch Swiss chard, thinly sliced
3 eggs, beaten
1-1/4 c. half-and-half
1/8 t. dried thyme
salt and pepper to taste
1 c. shredded Cheddar cheese

In a large oven-proof skillet over medium-high heat, cook bacon until crisp. Drain bacon on paper towels; reserve drippings. In one tablespoon drippings, sauté onion, red pepper and corn for 5 minutes. Add beans; sauté another 3 minutes. Transfer vegetable mixture to a bowl; set aside. Add one teaspoon drippings to skillet; sauté chard for 2 minutes. Add to vegetable mixture in bowl. In a separate large bowl, whisk eggs, half-and-half and seasonings. Stir in bacon, cheese and vegetable mixture; pour into skillet. Bake at 375 degrees for about 35 minutes, until set and crust is golden. Let stand for 10 minutes; cut into squares.

Jo Ann's Garden Frittata

Sonya Labbe, Santa Monica, CA

Hashbrown Quiche

A hearty quiche baked in a crust of hashbrowns! Enjoy it for breakfast, or add a zesty salad and have breakfast for dinner.

Serves 4 to 6

3 c. frozen shredded hashbrowns, thawed
1/4 c. butter, melted
3 eggs, beaten
1 c. half-and-half
3/4 c. cooked ham, diced
1/2 c. green onions, chopped
1 c. shredded Cheddar cheese
salt and pepper to taste

In a cast-iron skillet, combine hashbrowns and butter. Press into the bottom and up the sides of skillet. Transfer the skillet to oven. Bake, uncovered, at 450 degrees for 20 to 25 minutes, until crisp and golden. Remove from oven; cool slightly. Combine remaining ingredients in a bowl; pour mixture over the hashbrowns. Reduce the oven temperature to 350 degrees. Bake for another 30 minutes, or until quiche is golden and set.

Renae Scheiderer, Beallsville, OH

Festive Brunch Frittata

Serve this delicious egg dish in the skillet that you cook it in for a fun and rustic look.

Serves 6

8 eggs, beaten
1/2 t. salt
1/8 t. pepper
1/2 c. shredded Cheddar cheese
2 T. butter
2 c. red, green and yellow peppers, chopped
1/4 c. onion, chopped
Garnish: chopped fresh parsley

Beat together eggs, salt and pepper. Fold in cheese and set aside. Melt butter over medium heat in a 10" non-stick, oven-safe skillet. Add peppers and onion to skillet; sauté until tender. Pour eggs over peppers and onion; don't stir. Cover and cook over medium-low heat for about 9 minutes. Eggs are set when frittata is lightly golden on the underside. Turn oven on broil. Move skillet from stovetop to oven; broil top about 5 inches from heat until lightly golden. Garnish with parsley.

Festive Brunch Frittata

Megan Brooks, Antioch, TN

Skillet Strawberry Jam

Try your hand at jam-making with this simple recipe...your family will be so pleased, and so will you!

Makes about 1-1/2 cups

4 c. strawberries, hulled and
   crushed
1/2 c. sugar
1 T. lemon juice
Optional: 1/4 t. vanilla extract

Combine strawberries, sugar and lemon juice in a cast-iron skillet over medium-high heat; mix well. Cook, stirring often, until strawberries soften and mixture thickens, about 10 minutes. Remove from heat; stir in vanilla, if using. Store in an airtight jar in refrigerator for up to 3 weeks.

Donna Wilson, Maryville, TN

Glazed Pumpkin Scones

I absolutely love pumpkin and scones! These smell so yummy when baking, and taste even better when done. One of my sneaky ways to get kids to eat vegetables.

Makes 8 scones

2 c. all-purpose flour
1/2 c. sugar
1 T. baking powder
1/2 t. salt
1-1/2 t. pumpkin pie spice
1/2 c. butter, diced
1/2 c. canned pumpkin
3 T. milk
1 egg, beaten

Combine flour, sugar, baking powder, salt and spice in a large bowl. Cut in butter with a pastry blender until crumbly; set aside. In a separate bowl, whisk together pumpkin, milk and egg. Fold pumpkin mixture into flour mixture. Form dough into a ball; pat out dough onto a floured surface. Form into a 9-inch circle. Cut into 8 wedges and place on a greased baking sheet. Bake at 425 degrees for 14 to 16 minutes. Drizzle scones with Powdered Sugar Glaze; allow to set.

Powdered Sugar Glaze:
1 c. powdered sugar
2 to 3 T. milk
1/2 t. pumpkin pie spice

Mix all ingredients together, adding enough milk for a drizzling consistency.

Glazed Pumpkin Scones

Jennifer Rose Blay, Puyallup, WA

Jennifer's BBQ Scrambled Eggs

My dad taught me to put barbecue sauce in scrambled eggs as a special treat. Along with the herbs and spices, the sauce gives these eggs a wonderful flavor. I hope you and your family enjoy this recipe as much as my husband and I do!

Makes 4 servings

8 eggs, beaten
1/4 c. half-and-half
4 t. hickory barbecue sauce
1 t. dried parsley
1/2 t. dried basil
1/2 t. garlic powder
1/2 t. onion powder
1/2 t. celery salt
1/4 t. salt, or to taste
1/4 t. pepper, or to taste
1/8 t. cayenne pepper
1 T. butter
Optional: shredded Cheddar cheese

In a large bowl, whisk together eggs, half-and-half, barbecue sauce and seasonings; set aside. Melt butter in a large skillet over medium heat; pour egg mixture into skillet. Scramble eggs over medium-low to medium heat to desired consistency. If desired, sprinkle with shredded cheese just before serving.

Wendy Paffenroth, Pine Island, NY

Apple-Stuffed French Toast

Treat your family to this delectable French toast, filled with brown sugar-sweetened apples.

Makes 4 servings

3 apples, peeled, cored and cut
    into chunks
1/4 c. brown sugar, packed
cinnamon to taste
2 eggs, beaten
1/2 c. milk
1 t. vanilla extract
8 slices wheat bread
Garnish: maple syrup

In a saucepan, combine apples, brown sugar, cinnamon and a small amount of water. Cover and simmer over medium-low heat for 5 to 10 minutes, until apples are soft; set aside. Meanwhile, in a separate bowl, whisk together eggs, milk and vanilla. Heat a greased cast-iron skillet over medium heat. Quickly dip bread into egg mixture, coating both sides; place in skillet. Cook until golden on both sides. To serve, place one slice of French toast on a plate; top with a scoop of apple mixture and another slice of French toast. Drizzle with maple syrup.

Apple-Stuffed French Toast

Pam Hooley, LaGrange, IN

Stir & Go Biscuits & Sausage Gravy

This is a quick, stick-to-your-ribs meal...sometimes I'll even serve it for supper. Since finding this recipe for biscuits made with oil, rather than shortening, I make them more often, and the gravy is so easy to make too.

Serves 4 to 6

2 c. all-purpose flour
2-1/2 t. baking powder
1/8 t. baking soda
1 t. sugar
1 t. salt
1 c. buttermilk
1/2 c. oil
Garnish: melted butter

In a large bowl, stir together flour, baking powder, baking soda, sugar and salt. Add buttermilk and oil; stir until moistened. Roll out dough on a floured surface. Cut dough with a biscuit cutter, or drop dough by half cupfuls, onto an ungreased baking sheet. Bake at 425 degrees for about 15 minutes; brush with butter. While biscuits are baking, make Sausage Gravy. Serve gravy over hot biscuits.

Sausage Gravy:
1 lb. ground pork breakfast sausage
2 T. all-purpose flour
1/2 c. milk
salt and pepper to taste

Brown sausage in a skillet over medium heat. Drain; stir in flour until mixed well. Add milk; cook and stir until thickened. May add more milk to desired consistency. Season with salt and pepper.

Vickie, Gooseberry Patch

Fiesta Corn Tortilla Quiche

Use hot or mild sausage...the choice is up to you.

Serves 4

1 lb. ground pork sausage
5 6-inch corn tortillas
4-oz. can chopped green chiles, drained
1 c. shredded Monterey Jack cheese
1 c. shredded Cheddar cheese
6 eggs, beaten
1/2 c. whipping cream
1/2 c. small-curd cottage cheese

Brown sausage in a cast-iron skillet over medium heat; drain. Set sausage aside; wipe skillet clean. Arrange tortillas in the same skillet, overlapping on the bottom and extending up the sides. Spoon sausage, chiles and cheeses into tortilla-lined skillet. In a bowl, beat together remaining ingredients. Pour egg mixture over sausage mixture. Transfer skillet to oven. Bake, uncovered, at 375 degrees for 45 minutes, or until golden. Cut into wedges to serve.

Fiesta Corn Tortilla Quiche

Sherri Hagel, Spokane, WA

Melt-In-Your-Mouth Biscuits

Split and served with butter and jam or topped with sausage gravy, these flaky biscuits live up to their name!

Makes one to 2 dozen

1-1/2 c. all-purpose flour
1/2 c. whole-wheat flour
4 t. baking powder
1/2 t. salt
2 T. sugar
1/4 c. chilled butter, sliced
1/4 c. shortening
2/3 c. milk
1 egg, beaten

In a large bowl, sift flours, baking powder, salt and sugar together; cut in butter and shortening. Add milk; stir in egg. Knead on a floured surface until smooth; roll out to 1/2-inch thickness. Cut with a biscuit cutter; place biscuits on ungreased baking sheets. Bake at 450 degrees for 10 to 15 minutes, until golden.

Jennifer Hansen, Escanaba, MI

Sunrise Granola

Carry this amazing granola with you on an early morning hike! It will give you energy and it tastes super-good as well!

Makes one dozen

1 c. long-cooking oats, uncooked
1/4 c. unsweetened flaked coconut
2 T. sunflower seeds
1/4 c. wheat germ
1/4 t. cinnamon
1 T. honey
1/4 t. vanilla extract
2 t. canola oil

In a large mixing bowl, combine oats, coconut, sunflower seeds, wheat germ and cinnamon. In a separate bowl, combine honey, vanilla and oil; blend well. Pour honey mixture into oat mixture; blend well. Spread on a baking sheet and bake at 350 degrees for 20 to 25 minutes, stirring every 5 minutes. Let cool, then store in an airtight jar.

Sunrise Granola

Vickie, Gooseberry Patch

Farmers' Market Omelet

I love visiting the farmers' market bright & early on Saturday mornings... a terrific way to begin the day!

Serves one

1 t. olive oil
1 slice bacon, diced
2 T. onion, chopped
2 T. zucchini, diced
5 cherry tomatoes, quartered
1/2 t. fresh thyme, minced
3 eggs, beaten
1/4 c. fontina cheese, shredded

Heat oil in a skillet over medium-high heat. Add bacon and onion; cook and stir until bacon is crisp and onion is tender. Add zucchini, tomatoes and thyme. Allow to cook until zucchini is soft and juice from tomatoes has slightly evaporated. Lower heat to medium and stir in eggs. Cook, lifting edges to allow uncooked egg to flow underneath. When eggs are almost fully cooked, sprinkle with cheese and fold over.

Mary Ann Lewis, Olive Branch, MS

Best-Ever Breakfast Bars

These chewy, healthy bars are perfect to grab in the morning for a perfect take-along breakfast.

Makes 12 bars, serves 12

1 c. Sunrise Granola (see page 36)
1 c. quick-cooking oats, uncooked
1/2 c. all-purpose flour
1/4 c. brown sugar, packed
1/8 t. cinnamon
1/2 c. unsalted mixed nuts, coarsely chopped
1/2 c. dried fruit, chopped into small pieces
2 T. ground flaxseed meal
1/4 c. canola oil
1/3 c. honey
1/2 t. vanilla extract
1 egg, beaten

Combine granola and the next 7 ingredients in a large bowl. Whisk together oil, honey and vanilla; stir into granola mixture. Add egg; stir to blend. Press mixture into a parchment paper-lined 9"x7" sheet pan. Bake at 325 degrees for 30 to 35 minutes, until lightly golden around the edges. Remove from oven and cool 30 minutes to one hour. Slice into bars.

Best-Ever Breakfast Bars

Beth Bundy, Long Prairie, MN

Quick Strawberry Cream Danish

These are super easy, super tasty and super pretty. A couple of these with your coffee will definitely make your morning bright!

Makes 16

2 8-oz. pkgs. cream cheese, softened
1 egg, separated
1 t. vanilla extract
1 t. lemon juice
1 T. all-purpose flour
2 8-oz. tubes refrigerated crescent
   rolls
1/2 c. strawberry preserves, divided

Beat together cream cheese, egg yolk, vanilla, lemon juice and flour. Unroll and separate rolls; place a teaspoon of cream cheese mixture in the center of each triangle. Fold over edges of rolls, leaving center open. Brush with beaten egg white. Place on ungreased baking sheets. Bake at 350 degrees for 20 minutes. Remove from oven; cool slightly. Top each piece with a teaspoon of strawberry preserves.

Jo Ann, Gooseberry Patch

Herbed Mushroom Omelet

This savory omelet is sure to become a family favorite. I love to serve it with fresh tomatoes or fruit.

Serves 2

4 to 6 eggs, beaten
1 T. fresh parsley, chopped
1 t. fresh oregano, chopped
1/2 t. fresh thyme, chopped
salt and pepper to taste
2 t. butter, divided
1-1/2 c. sliced mushrooms

Whisk together eggs and seasonings; set aside. Melt one teaspoon butter in a skillet over medium heat. Add mushrooms and sauté until tender; remove from skillet and set aside. Melt 1/2 teaspoon butter in skillet over low heat; pour in half the egg mixture. Stir eggs around in skillet with a spatula to cook evenly. Lift edges to allow uncooked egg to flow underneath. When almost cooked, spoon on half the mushrooms and fold over. Repeat with remaining egg mixture.

Herbed Mushroom Omelet

Holly Jackson, St. George, UT

Ham & Feta Cheese Omelet

This omelet is so simple to make, it will become your go-to breakfast!

Serves one

2 eggs, beaten
1/4 c. crumbled feta cheese
1/4 c. cucumber, diced
2 T. green onion, chopped
1/4 c. cooked ham, cubed
salt and pepper to taste
Garnish: salsa

Combine all ingredients except salsa in a bowl; mix well. Pour into a lightly greased sauté pan or small skillet. Without stirring, cook over low heat until set. Fold over; transfer to serving plate. Serve with salsa.

Micki Stephens, Marion, OH

Rise & Shine Breakfast Pizza

You will enjoy tasting the layers of all your breakfast favorites in this dish!

Serves 8 to 10

2-lb. pkg. frozen shredded
    hashbrowns
1-1/2 c. shredded Cheddar cheese,
    divided
7 eggs, beaten
1/2 c. milk
salt and pepper to taste
10 to 12 pork breakfast sausage
    patties, cooked

Prepare hashbrowns according to package directions; spread on an ungreased baking sheet or pizza pan. Top with 1/2 cup cheese; set aside. Whisk together eggs and milk in a microwave-safe bowl; microwave on high 3 minutes, then scramble eggs well with a whisk. Return to microwave and cook 3 more minutes; whisk well to scramble. Layer eggs on top of cheese; add salt and pepper to taste. Top with remaining cheese. Arrange sausage patties on top. Bake at 400 degrees for 10 minutes, or until cheese is melted. Cut into squares or wedges to serve.

Rise & Shine Breakfast Pizza

Jackie Smulski, Lyons, IL

Scrambled Eggs & Lox

These eggs are sure to please everyone...they're excellent with toasted English muffins or bagels.

Serves 3

6 eggs, beaten
1 T. fresh dill, minced
1 T. fresh chives, minced
1 T. green onion, minced
pepper to taste
2 T. butter
4-oz. pkg. smoked salmon, diced

Whisk together eggs, herbs, onion and pepper. Melt butter in a large skillet over medium heat. Add egg mixture and stir gently with a spatula until eggs begin to set. Stir in salmon; continue cooking until eggs reach desired doneness.

Gloria Heigh, Santa Fe, NM

Quinoa Bowls with Swiss Chard & Poached Egg

This dish is filled with so much texture and flavor. Our family has learned to love quinoa in so many recipes!

Makes 2 servings

3 T. olive oil, divided
1/2 onion, chopped
1 carrot, peeled and sliced
1 bunch Swiss chard, stems chopped
    and leaves torn, divided
1 clove garlic, minced
1 c. sliced mushrooms
2 T. water
1 t. salt
1 c. cooked quinoa, warmed
2 t. vinegar
2 eggs
pepper to taste
2 T. fresh chives, chopped

Heat one tablespoon oil in a skillet over medium-high heat. Add onion, carrot and Swiss chard stems; cook, stirring often, until softened. Add garlic and mushrooms; cook until mushrooms are softened, adding more oil if needed. Place chard leaves on top of onion mixture; add 2 tablespoons water and salt. Cover and cook until leaves wilt, about 2 minutes; stir in quinoa. Divide mixture between 2 bowls; set aside. To a saucepan over medium heat, add vinegar and 2 inches water; bring to a simmer. Crack one egg into a saucer. Using a slotted spoon, swirl simmering water in a circle; slowly add egg. Cook until yolk is softly set. Remove with a slotted spoon and place on top of one quinoa bowl. Repeat with second egg. Drizzle each bowl with one tablespoon remaining oil; sprinkle with pepper and chives.

Quinoa Bowls with Swiss Chard & Poached Egg

Leslie Williams, Americus, GA

Maple Pecan Brunch Ring

A sweet & simple way to make a tasty treat for guests.

Makes about 12 servings

3/4 c. chopped pecans
1/2 c. brown sugar, packed
2 t. cinnamon
2 17.3-oz. tubes refrigerated
   jumbo flaky biscuits
2 T. butter, melted
1/2 c. maple syrup

Combine pecans, brown sugar and cinnamon; set aside. Split each biscuit horizontally; brush half of the biscuits with butter and sprinkle with half the pecan mixture. Arrange topped biscuits in a circle on an ungreased baking sheet; overlap each biscuit slightly and keep within 2 inches of the edge of the baking sheet. Brush remaining biscuit halves with melted butter; sprinkle with remaining pecan mixture. Arrange a second ring just inside the first ring, overlapping edges. Bake at 350 degrees for 30 to 35 minutes, until golden. Remove to wire rack; cool 10 minutes. Brush lightly with maple syrup.

Julie Ann Perkins, Anderson, IN

Peanut Butter French Toast

Who can resist the classic taste of peanut butter & jelly?

Serves 2

4 slices white or whole-wheat bread
1/2 c. creamy peanut butter
2 T. grape jelly
3 eggs, beaten
1/4 c. milk
2 T. butter
Garnish: powdered sugar

Use bread, peanut butter and jelly to make 2 sandwiches; set aside. In a bowl, whisk together eggs and milk. Dip each sandwich into egg mixture. Melt butter in a non-stick skillet over medium heat. Add sandwiches to skillet and cook until golden, about 2 to 3 minutes on each side. Sprinkle with powdered sugar; cut diagonally into triangles.

Peanut Butter French Toast

Jill Ball, Highland, UT

Breakfast Bruschetta

My family loves bruschetta...and now they can have it for breakfast!

Serves 4

1 c. red or green grapes, sliced
1 c. strawberries, hulled and sliced
1/4 t. cinnamon
1/8 t. nutmeg
1 c. cottage or ricotta cheese
1 T. chopped walnuts
1 baguette, cut in half lengthwise
   and sliced into 1-inch diagonals
2 to 3 T. olive oil

Place fruit in a small bowl; sprinkle with cinnamon and nutmeg. In another bowl, mix cheese and nuts. Brush bread lightly with olive oil and place on an ungreased baking sheet. Bake at 450 degrees until the bread turns golden, abut 3 minutes. Remove from oven and spread cheese mixture on each piece of bread. Top with fruit mixture.

Linda Bonwill, Englewood, FL

Spinach & Tomato French Toast

This one-slice version is a less-carb way to make French toast...plus, it looks so pretty!

Serves 4

3 eggs
salt and pepper to taste
8 slices Italian bread
4 c. fresh spinach, torn
2 tomatoes, sliced
shaved Parmesan cheese

In a bowl, beat eggs with salt and pepper. Dip bread slices into egg mixture. Place in a lightly greased skillet over medium heat; cook one side until lightly golden. Place fresh spinach, tomato slice and cheese onto each slice, pressing lightly to secure on the bread. Flip and briefly cook on other side until cooked. Flip over and serve open face.

Spinach & Tomato French Toast

Elizabeth Holcomb, Canyon Lake, TX

Texas Toads in the Hole

I made this breakfast for my girls when they were little. They always loved it because of the funny name, as well as the fact they had eggs and toast all in one dish!

Serves 4

2 T. butter
4 slices Texas toast
4 eggs
salt and pepper to taste
Optional: jam, jelly or preserves

Spread butter on both sides of Texas toast. Using a biscuit cutter, cut a circle out of the middle of each slice of toast; set aside rounds. Place toast slices in a large, lightly greased skillet over medium heat; break an egg into each hole. Season with salt and pepper. Cook until egg white begins to set, then carefully flip. Continue to cook until eggs reach desired doneness. In a separate skillet, toast reserved bread rounds. Top rounds with jam, jelly or preserves, if desired. Serve with toast slices.

Linda Picard, Newport, OR

Savory Oatmeal Bowls with Egg, Bacon & Kale

This one-bowl breakfast will give you a jump-start for a busy day at school or work.

Serves 2

2 slices bacon, diced
1 bunch kale, thinly sliced
1/2 c. tomato, diced
1 t. red wine vinegar
1/8 t. salt
1 c. cooked steel-cut oats
1/3 c. avocado, peeled, pitted
    and diced
1 t. olive oil
2 eggs
1/8 t. pepper
Optional: 1/2 t. hot pepper sauce

In a large skillet over medium heat, cook bacon until almost crisp, stirring occasionally. Add kale; cook for 2 to 4 minutes, until wilted. Stir in tomato, vinegar and salt. Divide oats evenly between 2 bowls. Top with kale mixture and avocado; set aside. Wipe skillet clean with a paper towel; return to medium heat. Add oil and swirl to coat. Crack eggs into skillet, one at a time; cook for 2 minutes. Cover and cook for one minute, or until whites are set. Top each bowl with one egg. Sprinkle with pepper and hot sauce, if using.

Savory Oatmeal Bowls with Egg, Bacon & Kale

Dale Duncan, Waterloo, IA

Bacon & Egg Potato Skins

A tummy-filling complete meal in a potato skin...yummy!

Makes 4 servings

2 baking potatoes
4 eggs, beaten
1 to 2 t. butter
salt and pepper to taste
1/4 c. shredded Monterey Jack
   cheese
1/4 c. shredded Cheddar cheese
4 slices bacon, crisply cooked
   and crumbled
Garnish: sour cream, chopped
   fresh chives

Bake potatoes at 400 degrees for one hour, until tender. Slice potatoes in half lengthwise; scoop out centers and reserve for another recipe. Place potato skins on a lightly greased baking sheet. Bake at 400 degrees for 6 to 8 minutes, until crisp. In a skillet over medium heat, scramble eggs in butter just until they begin to set. Add salt and pepper; remove from heat. Spoon equal amounts of eggs, cheeses and bacon into each potato skin. Reduce heat to 350 degrees and bake for 7 to 10 minutes, until cheese is melted and eggs are completely set. Garnish with sour cream and chives.

Rita Morgan, Pueblo, CO

Southwestern Flatbread

Yum...hot fresh-baked bread to enjoy for breakfast with a cup of fresh fruit! Easy to change up to Italian flavors too, with oregano and Parmesan cheese.

Makes about 15 pieces

2 t. olive oil, divided
11-oz. tube refrigerated crusty
   French loaf
1/2 c. roasted sunflower kernels
1 t. chili powder
1/2 to 1 t. coarse salt

Brush a 15"x10" sheet pan with one teaspoon oil; unroll dough onto pan. Use a floured rolling pin to roll out into a rectangle. Drizzle dough with remaining oil; brush over dough. In a small bowl, combine sunflower kernels and chili powder; mix well and sprinkle over the dough. Firmly press sunflower kernels into dough; sprinkle top with salt. Bake at 375 degrees for 12 to 16 minutes, until golden. Remove flatbread to a wire rack; cool 10 minutes. Tear or cut into pieces.

Southwestern Flatbread

Jo Ann, Gooseberry Patch

Blueberry-Lemon Crepes

A scrumptious, impressive and refreshing breakfast!

Makes 6 servings

3-oz. pkg. cream cheese, softened
1-1/2 c. half-and-half
1 T. lemon juice
3-3/4 oz. pkg. instant lemon
    pudding mix
1/2 c. biscuit baking mix
1 egg
6 T. milk
1 c. blueberry pie filling

Combine cream cheese, half-and-half, lemon juice and dry pudding mix in a bowl. Beat with an electric mixer on low speed for 2 minutes. Refrigerate for 30 minutes. Lightly grease a 6" skillet and place over medium-high heat. In a bowl, combine biscuit baking mix, egg and milk. Beat until smooth. Pour 2 tablespoons of batter into skillet for each crepe. Rotating the skillet quickly, allow batter to cover the bottom of the skillet. Cook each crepe until lightly golden, then flip, cooking again until just golden. Spoon 2 tablespoonfuls of cream cheese mixture onto each crepe and roll up. Top with remaining cream cheese mixture and pie filling.

Dale Duncan, Waterloo, IA

Rise & Shine Sandwiches

My family loves these breakfast sandwiches anytime! They're easy to make and easy to adapt to your own tastes.

Makes 8 servings

2-1/4 c. buttermilk biscuit
    baking mix
1/2 c. water
8 pork sausage breakfast patties
8 eggs, beaten
1 T. butter
salt and pepper to taste
8 slices American cheese

In a bowl, combine biscuit mix with water; stir until just blended. Turn onto a floured surface and knead for one minute. Roll dough out to 1/2-inch thickness. Cut out 8 biscuits with a 3-inch round biscuit cutter. Arrange on an ungreased baking sheet. Bake at 425 degrees for 8 to 10 minutes, until golden. Meanwhile, in a skillet over medium heat, brown and cook sausage patties; drain. In a separate skillet over low heat, scramble eggs in butter to desired doneness; season with salt and pepper. Split biscuits; top each biscuit bottom with a sausage patty, a spoonful of eggs and a cheese slice. Add biscuit tops and serve.

Rise & Shine Sandwiches

Mini Deep-Dish Pizzas

CHAPTER TWO

NO-FUSS
Appetizers
& Snacks

Feta Squares, Page 60

Simple Stromboli, Page 86

Amy Coats, Savannah, MO

Crunchy Chicken Rolls

This recipe is always a hit with family & friends. I got this recipe in a high school cooking class and have been using it ever since! For a little variety, I like to replace the plain cream cheese with the garlic & herb kind.

Serves 6 to 8

12-oz. can chicken, drained
   and flaked
2 8-oz. pkgs. cream cheese, softened
3 T. fresh chives, chopped
2 8-oz. tubes refrigerated
   crescent rolls
2 T. butter, melted
4 c. chicken stuffing mix

In a large bowl, combine chicken, cream cheese and chives; blend well and set aside. Separate and flatten crescent rolls; top each triangle with one tablespoon of chicken mixture. Roll up triangles, sealing well. Dip each triangle into melted butter, then into stuffing mix. Place rolls on a greased baking sheet, stuffing-side up. Bake at 350 degrees for 10 to 15 minutes, until lightly golden.

Ann Tober, Biscoe, AZ

Prosciutto-Wrapped Asparagus

This simple and pretty presentation of asparagus is always a hit at any party or event.

Serves 6

1 bunch asparagus, about 10 pieces,
   trimmed
1 T. olive oil
1 t. kosher salt
1 t. pepper
3-oz. pkg. sliced prosciutto, cut into
   strips with fat removed
Optional: lemon slices

Toss asparagus with oil, salt and pepper. Arrange in a single layer on an ungreased rimmed baking sheet. Bake at 400 degrees for 5 minutes. Allow to cool slightly. Wrap each asparagus spear with a strip of prosciutto. Return to oven and bake for 4 more minutes or until asparagus is crisp-tender and prosciutto is slightly browned. Serve warm or at room temperature, garnished with thin lemon slices, if desired.

Prosciutto-Wrapped Asparagus

Jen Sell, Farmington, MN

Seasoned Oyster Crackers

So good by themselves or sprinkled into homemade soups and stews.

Makes 24 servings

1-1/2 c. oil
2 1-oz. pkgs. ranch salad dressing mix
1 T. lemon pepper
1 T. dill weed
2 10-oz. pkgs. oyster crackers

Whisk first 4 ingredients together; pour over oyster crackers. Toss gently; spread on an ungreased baking sheet. Bake at 225 degrees for one hour, stirring every 15 minutes.

Carla Whitfield, Bonham, TX

Stuffed Jalapeños

I wanted to make stuffed jalapeños for my husband. I had never made them before and he always enjoyed them when other people made them so I came up with this...he loves them!

Makes 10 servings

10 large jalapeño peppers
1-1/2 c. shredded Cheddar cheese
2 12-oz. cans chicken, partially drained
1-1/4 oz. pkg. taco seasoning mix
10 slices bacon

Cut each jalapeño pepper across the top; cut a slit and open up pepper. Remove seeds and membranes; set side. In a bowl, combine cheese, chicken and taco seasoning; mix well. Stuff peppers with mixture. Wrap each with a bacon slice; use a wooden toothpick to fasten. Place peppers on an ungreased baking sheet. Bake at 325 degrees for 40 to 45 minutes, until peppers are soft and bacon is chewy.

Jane Kirsch, Weymouth, MA

Feta Squares

These tasty little goodies are so easy to make and go fast!

Serves 8 to 10

8-oz container crumbled feta cheese
8-oz. pkg. cream cheese, softened
2 T. olive oil
3 cloves garlic, finely chopped
1 loaf sliced party pumpernickel bread
1 pt. grape tomatoes, halved
2 to 3 T. fresh chives, finely chopped

In a bowl, mix feta cheese, cream cheese, olive oil and garlic. Spread mixture on pumpernickel bread slices. Place on ungreased baking sheets. Top each square with a tomato half; sprinkle with chives. Bake at 350 degrees for 15 minutes.

Feta Squares

Cathy Siebrecht, Des Moines, IA

Spicy Garlic Almonds

If you like almonds, you'll love this recipe with garlic and a kick of red pepper.

Makes about 3 cups

2 T. low-sodium soy sauce
2 t. hot pepper sauce
2 cloves garlic, pressed
1 lb. blanched whole almonds
1 T. butter, melted
1 t. pepper
1/4 t. red pepper flakes

Combine sauces and garlic in a medium bowl. Add almonds, stirring until well coated. Brush butter over a 15"x10" sheet pan. Spread almonds on pan in a single layer. Bake at 350 degrees for 10 minutes. Sprinkle salt and peppers over almonds; return to oven for 15 minutes. Remove from oven; cool on pan. Store in an airtight container.

Irene Robinson, Cincinnati, OH

Harvest Moon Popcorn

This is a great snack to have on hand instead of cereal mix. It's also terrific for lunchboxes.

Makes about 10 cups

8 c. popped popcorn
2 c. canned shoestring potatoes
1/2 c. butter, melted
1 t. Worcestershire sauce
1 t. lemon pepper seasoning
1 t. dried dill weed
1/2 t. onion powder
1/2 t. garlic powder
1/4 t. salt

Combine popcorn and potatoes in a large bowl; set aside. In a separate small bowl, stir together remaining ingredients. Drizzle butter mixture over popcorn mixture; toss to coat. Spread on a rimmed baking sheet. Bake, uncovered, at 350 degrees for 8 to 10 minutes. Cool; store in an airtight container.

Harvest Moon Popcorn

Beverley Williams, San Antonio, TX

Batter-Fried Mushrooms

I wanted a tasty appetizer and came up with these delicious gems. They are the first thing to go at parties!

Serves 4 to 6

1 c. all-purpose flour
1/2 c. cornstarch
1 T. grated Parmesan cheese
3/4 t. baking powder
1/2 t. garlic powder
1/2 t. Italian seasoning
1/2 t. dried thyme
1/8 t. cayenne pepper
1/8 t. salt
1/4 t. pepper
1 c. buttermilk
2 c. panko bread crumbs
10-oz. pkg. cremini mushrooms, stems trimmed
vegetable oil for frying
Garnish: favorite dipping sauce or ranch salad dressing

In a shallow dish, combine flour, cornstarch, Parmesan cheese, baking powder and seasonings; mix well. Add buttermilk; stir to form batter. Place bread crumbs in a separate shallow dish. Dip mushrooms into batter; let excess drip off. Roll mushrooms in bread crumbs to coat. Heat one inch vegetable oil in a skillet over medium heat. Working in batches, use tongs to carefully add mushrooms to hot oil; do not crowd the mushrooms. Cook, turning mushrooms occasionally, for 7 to 10 minutes, until golden. Gently remove mushrooms to a paper towel-lined plate. Allow to cool for 2 to 5 minutes. Serve with dipping sauce or ranch dressing.

Tracey Zimmerman, Spirit Lake, IA

Chili Sweet Potato Fries

This is a great way to get the kids to eat sweet potatoes. They will love them!

Serves 10

3-1/2 lbs. sweet potatoes, sliced into 1-inch wedges
2 T. olive oil
3/4 t. salt
1/4 t. pepper
1/2 c. orange juice
1 T. honey
2 t. chili powder

Place potato wedges in a large plastic zipping bag; sprinkle with oil, salt and pepper. Toss to mix. Arrange potato wedges on lightly greased baking sheets. Stir together orange juice, honey and chili powder; set aside. Bake, uncovered, at 450 degrees for 25 to 30 minutes, until tender, shaking pans and basting with orange juice mixture several times.

Chili Sweet Potato Fries

Stephanie Schmidt, Las Vegas, NV

Pita Chips

So simple to make and everyone always loves them!

Serves 8

4 6-inch whole-wheat pita rounds, split
6 t. olive oil
2 cloves garlic, pressed

Cut each split pita round in half; cut each half into 4 triangles. In a small bowl, combine olive oil and garlic in a small bowl; brush over triangles. Arrange triangles in a single layer on an ungreased baking sheet. Bake at 350 degrees for 8 to 10 minutes, until crisp and golden.

Sharon Hamill, Douglassville, PA

Tuna Wrap-Ups

This is our family's variation on pigs in a blanket. The kids usually fight over the last one! Create a best-loved appetizer with just a can of tuna and a few items from the fridge.

Makes 8 rolls, serves 8

6-oz. can tuna, drained
2 T. mayonnaise
salt and pepper to taste
8-oz. tube refrigerated crescent rolls, separated
4 slices American cheese

Mix tuna, mayonnaise, salt and pepper; set aside. Arrange crescents on an ungreased baking sheet; set aside. Fold cheese slices diagonally and break into 2 pieces; place one piece on each crescent. Spread one heaping tablespoon tuna mixture over cheese; roll up crescent rolls. Bake at 375 degrees for 12 minutes.

Cindy Skinner, Hagerstown, MD

Crab-Stuffed Mushrooms

The whole-grain bread gives these stuffed mushrooms great color.

Serves 15

15 mushrooms
7-oz. can crabmeat, drained and flaked
1 slice whole-grain bread, torn
1 egg, beaten
1/3 c. onion, chopped
salt and pepper to taste
2 T. grated Parmesan cheese
2 T. butter, melted

Remove and chop mushroom stems, setting aside mushroom caps. Combine chopped stems with crabmeat, bread, egg, onion and seasonings; mix well. Spoon mixture into mushroom caps; sprinkle with cheese and set aside. Brush melted butter over a 13"x9" sheet pan; arrange mushroom caps on pan. Broil for 2 to 4 minutes, until golden and heated through.

Crab-Stuffed Mushrooms

Marsha Baker, Pioneer OH

Pineapple-Ham Crescents

I found this delectable recipe in my mom's files after she had passed away. It has become a favorite, for more reasons than one. She used canned pineapple spears which aren't easy to find anymore, but pineapple chunks work well.

Makes 8

8-oz. tube refrigerated crescent rolls
8 thin slices deli ham, 2 inches wide
8 slices Swiss cheese, 2 inches wide
20-oz. can pineapple chunks or
    tidbits, drained, juice reserved
    and divided
1 T. Dijon mustard

Unroll crescent rolls; set aside. Wrap one strip of ham and one strip of cheese around 2 pineapple chunks or 2 to 3 tidbits. Place on the widest part of a crescent roll; roll up. Repeat; arrange on baking sheet. Bake at 375 degrees for 12 to 15 minutes, until golden. Meanwhile, combine mustard and reserved juice in a saucepan. Cook over medium-high heat until thickened, stirring frequently, about 10 minutes. Chop desired amount of remaining pineapple; stir into sauce. Serve sauce with crescents.

Rhonda Johnson, Studio City, CA

Bruschetta with Cranberry Relish

I love these bruschetta because they taste so good, but also because they are so pretty!

Serves 16

1 large whole-grain baguette loaf,
    sliced 1/4-inch thick
1 to 2 T. olive oil
1 t. orange zest
1 t. lemon zest
1/2 c. chopped pecans
1/2 c. crumbled low-fat blue cheese

Brush baguette slices lightly with oil. Arrange on a sheet pan; toast lightly under broiler. Turn slices over; spread with Cranberry Relish. Sprinkle with zests, pecans and blue cheese. Place under broiler just until cheese begins to melt.

Cranberry Relish:
16-oz. can whole-berry cranberry
    sauce
6-oz. pkg. sweetened dried
    cranberries
1/2 c. sugar
1 t. rum extract
1 c. chopped pecans

Stir all ingredients together.

Bruschetta with Cranberry Relish

Wendy Lee Paffenroth, Pine Island, NY

Seafood Pinwheels

Serve these with a fresh green salad and you almost have a meal!

Makes about 3 dozen

8-oz. pkg. cream cheese, softened
8-oz. pkg. imitation crabmeat, shredded
1/2 c. red pepper, chopped
1/2 c. shredded Cheddar cheese
2 green onions, chopped
1/4 c. fresh parsley, chopped
1/2 to 1 t. hot pepper sauce
chili powder to taste
6 6-inch flour tortillas
Garnish: paprika

Beat cream cheese until smooth; stir in crabmeat, red pepper, shredded cheese, onions, parsley and sauce. Sprinkle with chili powder; stir until well blended. Spread cheese mixture evenly over tortillas; roll up tightly. Slice off ends; wrap in plastic wrap. Refrigerate for 2 hours or overnight. When ready to serve, slice each roll into 6 slices. Arrange on a baking sheet sprayed with non-stick vegetable spray. Bake at 350 degrees for 10 to 12 minutes, until bubbly. Sprinkle with paprika; serve warm.

Cindy Elliott, Modesto, IL

Honey-Glazed Snack Mix

A perfect snack to munch while doing homework! This recipe is from my friend, Mary Beth Mitchell. I like the taste of this best when I use fresh honey from the farmers' market or orchard.

Makes about 10 cups

5 c. corn and rice cereal
3 c. mini pretzel twists
2 c. pecan halves
1/2 c. honey
1/2 c. butter, melted

Combine cereal, pretzels and pecans in a large bowl; set aside. Blend together honey and butter. Pour over cereal mixture; toss to coat. Spread on ungreased baking sheets. Bake at 300 degrees for 10 minutes. Stir and continue to bake an additional 10 to 15 minutes. Pour onto wax paper and cool completely. Store in airtight containers.

Honey-Glazed Snack Mix

Janae Mallonee, Marlborough, MA

Spinach & Feta Triangles

This was one of the first big projects my daughter Meredith took on in the kitchen. She loves spinach and feta cheese and wanted to recreate some little treats she had enjoyed in the past.

Makes one dozen

3 eggs, divided
1 T. water
10-oz. pkg. frozen chopped spinach, thawed and pressed dry
1 c. crumbled feta cheese
1 onion, finely chopped
1 sheet frozen phyllo dough, thawed

Whisk together one egg and water in a cup; set aside. In a bowl, mix remaining eggs, spinach, cheese and onion; set aside. Gently roll out dough on a floured surface; cut into 12 squares. Spoon spinach mixture evenly into the center of each square. Fold into triangles; press edges to seal. Brush egg mixture over triangle. Place triangles on a greased baking sheet. Bake at 400 degrees for 15 minutes, or until golden.

Lynn Williams, Muncie, IN

Pork & Apple Bites

We love party meatballs, but I was looking for something a little different. These are perfect for a fall tailgating party!

Makes about 3 dozen

1 lb. ground pork
1/4 t. cinnamon
1 t. salt
1/8 t. pepper
1/2 c. Granny Smith apple, peeled, cored and grated
1/4 c. soft rye bread crumbs
1/4 c. chopped walnuts
1/2 c. water
1/2 c. apple jelly

In a large bowl; combine pork and seasonings; mix well. Add apple, bread crumbs and walnuts; mix gently until well blended. Form mixture into balls by tablespoonfuls. Working in batches, brown meatballs in a large skillet over medium heat. Drain; return all meatballs to skillet. Pour water into skillet; cover tightly. Cook over medium-low heat for 15 minutes, or until meatballs are no longer pink in the center. Remove meatballs to a serving bowl; cover and set aside. Stir apple jelly into drippings in skillet; cook and stir until jelly is melted. Spoon sauce over meatballs.

Pork & Apple Bites

Melissa Dattoli, Richmond, VA

Cheesesteak Egg Rolls

One of my most-requested party recipes...everyone loves these! They require some prep but once you get the hang of wrapping them, the process goes quickly. Save time by making the filling a day ahead.

Makes 16 to 20

2 c. oil, divided
3/4 lb. deli rare roast beef, thinly
    sliced and finely chopped
1/2 onion, finely chopped
8 to 10 slices provolone cheese,
    cut in half
16 to 20 egg roll wrappers

Heat one tablespoon oil in a skillet over medium-high heat; add beef and onion. Cook, stirring occasionally, until beef is browned and onion is tender. Drain on paper towels; let cool for 10 minutes. (You may refrigerate if preparing ahead of time.) To assemble egg rolls, place an egg roll wrapper in front of you, in a diamond-shape direction. Place a half-slice of cheese horizontally in the center of the diamond; spoon a heaping 1/4 cup of beef filling over cheese. Set out a small glass of water. Gently lift up the bottom corner of wrapper, over the filling. With a moistened finger, dab a little water on the left and right corners of wrapper; fold each side in over the bottom corner. Dab a little water on the top corner; roll up the egg roll gently but firmly. Dab a little more water on the top corner to keep it closed. Repeat with remaining wrapper and filling. To a large skillet, add 1/2 to one inch remaining oil for frying. Heat over medium-high heat. Fry each egg roll for about 4 minutes per side until golden, adjusting heat as needed. Drain egg rolls on paper towels. Serve warm.

Carol Hickman, Kingsport, TN

Reuben Appetizers

Put these mini Reubens together in just a few minutes, and they'll be gone in seconds.

Serves 16

1 loaf sliced party rye bread
1/2 c. Thousand Island salad
    dressing
3/4 lb. sliced corned beef
14-oz. can sauerkraut, drained
1-1/2 c. shredded Swiss cheese

Spread bread slices on one side with dressing; set aside. Slice corned beef to fit bread; place 2 slices on each bread slice. Top with one to 2 teaspoons sauerkraut; sprinkle with cheese. Arrange on an ungreased baking sheet; bake at 350 degrees for 10 minutes or until cheese melts.

Reuben Appetizers

Ruth Cooksey, Plainfield, IN

Ruth's Swiss Bacon-Onion Dip

A yummy hot appetizer to serve with your favorite snack crackers.

Makes 4 cups

8 slices bacon
8-oz. pkg. cream cheese, softened
1 c. shredded Swiss cheese
1/2 c. mayonnaise
2 T. green onions, chopped
1 c. round buttery crackers, crushed

In a cast-iron skillet over medium-high heat, cook bacon until crisp. Remove bacon to paper towels. Drain skillet and wipe clean. Mix cheeses, mayonnaise and onion; spread in same skillet. Top with crumbled bacon and cracker crumbs. Transfer skillet to oven. Bake, uncovered, at 350 degrees for 15 to 20 minutes, until hot and bubbly.

Jo Ann, Gooseberry Patch

Baja Shrimp Quesadillas

These quesadillas are really so easy and so very yummy. Everyone always loves them!

Makes about 4 dozen

2-1/2 lbs. shrimp, peeled and cleaned
3 c. shredded Cheddar cheese
1/2 c. mayonnaise
3/4 c. salsa
1/4 t. ground cumin
1/4 t. cayenne pepper
1/4 t. pepper
12 6-inch flour tortillas

Chop shrimp, discarding tails. Mix shrimp, cheese, mayonnaise, salsa, cumin and peppers; spread one to 2 tablespoons on one tortilla. Place another tortilla on top; put on a greased baking sheet. Repeat with remaining tortillas. Bake at 350 degrees for 15 minutes; remove and cut into small triangles.

Baja Shrimp Quesadillas

Carmen Clever, Ashland, OH

Flaky Sausage Wraps

Use hot and spicy pork sausage if you want a little more kick to these wraps.

Makes 8

6-oz. pkg. ground pork sausage
1/4 c. onion, chopped
1/4 c. green pepper, chopped
1 clove garlic, minced
1/4 t. mustard
3-oz. pkg. cream cheese, softened
1 T. green onion, chopped
8-oz. tube refrigerated crescent
   rolls, separated

In a skillet over medium heat, brown sausage with onion, pepper and garlic; drain. Reduce heat; add mustard, cream cheese and green onion, stirring until cheese melts. Cool slightly; place in a food processor. Process until smooth; spread on crescent rolls. Roll up crescent-roll style; arrange on an ungreased baking sheet. Bake at 350 degrees for 10 to 12 minutes.

Cindy Shields, Issaquah, WI

Cheesy Spinach-Stuffed Mushrooms

I love to make these for parties, but I also make them when we have a movie night as a family. The entire family loves them and it makes the night super special.

Serves 12

10-oz. pkg. frozen chopped spinach,
   thawed and squeezed dry
1/4 c. cream cheese, softened
1 c. crumbled feta cheese
3/4 t. garlic powder
1/4 t. pepper
24 mushrooms, stems removed
1/2 c. grated Parmesan cheese

In a bowl, combine all ingredients except mushroom caps and Parmesan cheese; mix well. Spoon mixture into mushrooms; place on a rimmed baking sheet. Sprinkle mushrooms with Parmesan cheese. Bake at 350 degrees for 15 to 20 minutes, until bubbly and heated through. Serve warm.

Cheesy Spinach-Stuffed Mushrooms

Rogene Rogers, Bemidji, MN

Gingered Coconut Chicken Fingers

You can substitute Greek yogurt for the sour cream in the sauce if you want to watch your fat intake.

Serves 8

3/4 c. sweetened flaked coconut
3 T. plain dry bread crumbs
3/4 t. ground ginger
1/2 t cayenne pepper
2 T. honey
1 t. lemon or orange juice
14-oz. pkg. chicken tenders, sliced in
    half crosswise
salt to taste

In a blender or food processor, combine coconut, bread crumbs and spices. Pulse to blend; transfer to a shallow dish. Blend honey and juice in a separate shallow dish. Sprinkle chicken pieces with salt; coat in honey mixture and roll in coconut mixture. Place on baking sheet that has been sprayed with non-stick vegetable spray. Bake at 400 degrees for 12 to 15 minutes, until chicken is tender and no longer pink. Serve with Sour Cream Sauce.

Sour Cream Sauce:
1/3 c. sour cream
2 T. crushed pineapple with juice
1/4 t. ground ginger

Mix together in a small bowl.

Melissa Bordenkircher, Lake Worth, FL

Chinese Spareribs

Serve these at your next party and watch them disappear.

Serves 15

6 lbs. lean pork spareribs, sliced into
    serving-size portions
1/4 c. hoisin sauce
1/4 c. water
3 T. dry sherry
2 T. honey
1 T. low-sodium soy sauce
2 cloves garlic, minced

Place ribs in a very large plastic zipping bag. Mix remaining ingredients in a small bowl; pour over ribs. Seal bag; turn gently to coat ribs with marinade. Refrigerate for 6 hours to overnight, turning bag several times. Drain; reserve and refrigerate marinade. Place ribs on a lightly greased sheet pan. Cover with aluminum foil. Bake at 350 degrees for 1-1/2 hours. Uncover; brush reserved marinade over ribs, discarding any remaining marinade. Bake, uncovered, an additional 30 minutes, or until tender.

Chinese Spareribs

Robin Hill, Rochester, NY

Mushrooms Florentine

The nutmeg in this dish makes it so special.

Serves 10 to 12

16-oz. pkg. mushrooms, stems
    removed and chopped
2 T. butter, melted and divided
10-oz. pkg. frozen chopped spinach,
    cooked and drained
1/2 c. dry bread crumbs
1/2 t. garlic powder
1/8 t. nutmeg
salt and pepper to taste
1/2 c. grated Parmesan cheese,
    divided

Dip mushroom caps into one tablespoon melted butter. Place on an ungreased 13"x9" sheet pan; set aside. In a skillet over medium heat, sauté mushroom stems in remaining butter. Remove from heat. Add spinach, bread crumbs, seasonings and 1/4 cup cheese. Mix well and spoon into mushroom caps; sprinkle with remaining cheese. Bake, uncovered, at 350 degrees for 20 to 25 minutes. Serve hot.

Krista Marshall, Fort Wayne, IN

Mini Deep-Dish Pizzas

We love deep-dish pizza, but who has time to make it? These delicious bites make a fantastic appetizer.

Serves 12

15-oz. can pizza sauce
1/2 c. grated Parmesan cheese
1 T. Italian seasoning
4 large flour tortillas
1 c. shredded mozzarella cheese,
    divided
12 slices turkey pepperoni, quartered

In a small bowl, combine pizza sauce, Parmesan cheese and seasoning; stir well and set aside. Spray 12 muffin cups with non-stick vegetable spray. Using a glass tumbler, cut 3 rounds from each tortilla. Rounds should be just a little larger than muffin cups. Gently press tortilla rounds into muffin cups, covering each cup on the bottom and up the sides a little. Spoon 2 tablespoons sauce mixture into each cup; sprinkle with 1/2 cup mozzarella cheese. Top each cup with 4 pieces pepperoni. Bake at 400 degrees for about 10 minutes, until golden and crisp. Let stand 2 minutes; remove from muffin tin with a fork. Place on sheet pan and sprinkle remaining cheese on top; return to oven for a few minutes to melt cheese. Serve warm.

Mini Deep-Dish Pizzas

Jane Moore, Haverford, PA

Crab & Broccoli Rolls

Season these rolls with onion or garlic salt to taste, or spice them up with a dash of hot pepper sauce!

Makes 8 rolls, serves 8

6-oz. can flaked crabmeat, drained
10-oz. pkg. frozen chopped broccoli, cooked, drained and cooled
1/4 c. mayonnaise
1/2 c. shredded Swiss cheese
8-oz. tube refrigerated crescent rolls, separated

Combine crabmeat, broccoli, mayonnaise and cheese; spread about 2 tablespoons on each crescent. Roll up crescent roll-style; arrange on a lightly greased baking sheet. Bake at 375 degrees for 18 to 20 minutes.

Jessica Kraus, Delaware, OH

Jalapeño Popper Pinwheels

This is such a great recipe for football season!

Makes 8

4-oz. can diced jalapeño peppers, drained
8-oz. pkg. cream cheese, softened
1 c. shredded Mexican-blend cheese
2 t. salt
8-oz. tube refrigerated crescent rolls
grated Parmesan cheese to taste

In a large bowl, combine jalapeños, cheeses and salt; blend well and set aside. Unroll crescent rolls; seal seams but do not separate. Spread cream cheese mixture evenly over the dough. Roll up jelly-roll style; slice the roll into 1/3-inch slices. Arrange on a lightly greased baking sheet, leaving one inch between slices. Dust with Parmesan cheese. Bake at 375 degrees for 11 to 15 minutes, until tops begin to turn golden. Let cool for a minute, then transfer to a cooling rack.

Jalapeño Popper Pinwheels

Corrine Lane, Marysville, OH

Sausage & Parmesan Puffs

Bring along these puff pastries to a party, and they're sure to be a hit!

Makes 20 puffs, serves 10

2 frozen puff pastry shells, thawed
1 egg
1 T. milk
6 T. grated Parmesan cheese
1 lb. ground pork sausage

Cut each pastry shell lengthwise into 3 strips. In a small mixing bowl, beat egg with milk. Brush the top of pastry strips with half of the egg mixture; sprinkle one tablespoon cheese over each strip. Divide sausage into 6 parts and shape each into a log the same length as the strips. Place one sausage log into the middle of each strip. Fold edges up to enclose sausage and pinch edges together. Brush tops of rolls with remaining egg mixture. Chill for 15 minutes. Place a sheet of parchment paper on a baking sheet. Cut each pastry roll into one-inch sections and place on top of paper. Bake at 400 degrees for 15 to 20 minutes, until sausage is cooked and pastry is lightly golden.

Diane Williams, Mountain Top, PA

Simple Stromboli

I like ham in my stromboli, but my husband likes beef in his...so I make both kinds!

Serves 4

1 green pepper, thinly sliced
1 onion, thinly sliced
1 T. butter
13.8-oz. tube refrigerated pizza crust
1/2 lb. deli ham or roast beef, thinly sliced
8 slices mozzarella cheese
pepper to taste

In a skillet over medium heat, sauté green pepper and onion in butter until tender. Unroll unbaked pizza crust on a lightly greased baking sheet. Layer crust with slices of meat and cheese; top with green pepper mixture and season with pepper. Roll crust loosely into a tube, jelly-roll style; pinch top and sides closed. Bake, seam-side down, at 375 degrees for about 25 minutes, until golden. Slice to serve.

Simple Stromboli

Clarie Bertram, Lexington, KY

Oven-Toasted Potato Chips

Give these homemade potato chips a little more kick...sprinkle with Cajun or barbecue seasoning!

Serves 6

1 lb. new potatoes, sliced 1/8-inch
   thick
2 T. olive oil
1 t. salt, divided

Rinse sliced potatoes with very cold water; pat dry. Toss in oil and half of the salt. Spread in a single layer on an ungreased baking sheet. Bake at 500 degrees for 20 to 25 minutes, until golden. Sprinkle with remaining salt; serve warm.

Gladys Kielar, Whitehouse, OH

Caesar Toast Appetizers

These crispy, savory bites are ready in no time at all.

Serves 8

1 egg, beaten
1/4 c. Caesar salad dressing
8-oz. tube refrigerated crescent
   rolls, separated
2 c. herb-flavored stuffing mix,
   crushed
1/3 c. grated Parmesan cheese

Mix egg and salad dressing in a small bowl; set aside. Cut each crescent in half lengthwise, making 16 triangles. Dip triangles in egg mixture, then place in crushed stuffing to coat both sides. Place coated triangles one inch apart on an ungreased baking sheet. Sprinkle with Parmesan cheese. Bake at 375 degrees for 15 minutes.

Jordan Ray, Clermont, FL

Asian Chicken Wings

The cilantro in this recipe makes it one of my favorites.

Makes 2-1/2 to 3 dozen, serves 12

4 lbs. chicken wings
2 T. olive oil
1/2 t. salt
2 t. pepper, divided
1/4 c. honey
1 T. low-sodium soy sauce
1 t. Worcestershire sauce
juice of 1 lime
zest of 2 limes
2 cloves garlic, finely minced
1 T. fresh cilantro, chopped
2 t. red pepper flakes

Place wings on an aluminum foil-lined sheet pan. Drizzle wings with oil and toss to coat; sprinkle with salt and one teaspoon pepper. Bake at 400 degrees for 50 minutes; do not turn. Remove from oven. Using tongs, carefully lift wings from foil. Stir together pepper and other ingredients. Drizzle 1/3 cup of sauce mixture over hot wings and toss to coat. Serve remainder of sauce separately for dipping.

Asian Chicken Wings

Angie Walsh, Cedar Rapids, IA

Yummy Sausage Cups

We enjoy having these on Christmas day, but they're good any time of year. My mother-in-law makes them, and they are a huge hit!

Makes 5 dozen, serves 30

1 lb. maple-flavored ground
   pork breakfast sausage
8-oz. pkg. shredded sharp Cheddar
   cheese
16-oz. container sour cream
1-oz. pkg. ranch salad dressing mix
4 2.1-oz. pkgs. frozen phyllo cups

Brown sausage in a skillet over medium heat; drain and return to skillet. Stir in remaining ingredients except phyllo cups. Fill each phyllo cup with a scoop of sausage mixture. Arrange cups on ungreased baking sheets. Bake at 350 degrees for 15 minutes, or until heated through and cups are golden.

Nancy Kremkus, Ann Arbor, MI

Pepperoni Pizza Bites

Get creative and try this recipe with alternative toppings...you'll have a blast! So fun to make with the kids.

Makes 8 mini pizzas

11-oz. tube refrigerated thin
   pizza crust
1/2 c. pizza sauce
8 slices pepperoni
1/2 c. shredded mozzarella cheese

Do not unroll pizza crust; cut into 8 equal pieces. Arrange dough 3 inches apart on parchment-lined baking sheet. Flatten each piece of dough into a 2-inch circle. Spoon pizza sauce into each center. Top each pizza with pepperoni and cheese. Bake at 400 degrees for 12 minutes or until golden and cheese melts.

Pepperoni Pizza Bites

Michelle Powell, Valley, AL

Mexican Roasted Cauliflower

So quick and tasty...you'll make this recipe often!

Makes 6 servings

3 T. olive oil
3 cloves garlic, minced
1 T. chili powder, or to taste
1/2 t. dried cumin
1 lb. cauliflower, cut into bite-size
    flowerets
juice of 1 lime
1/4 c. fresh cilantro, chopped

Mix oil, garlic and spices in a large bowl. Add the cauliflower; toss to coat. Spread on an ungreased baking sheet. Bake, uncovered, at 325 degrees for one hour and 15 minutes, stirring occasionally. Remove from oven. Drizzle with lime juice; sprinkle with cilantro and toss well. Serve warm.

Jewel Grindey, Lindenhurst, IL

Seeded Tortilla Crisps

Serve these with your favorite dipping sauce for a fun and easy appetizer or snack.

Makes about 2-1/2 dozen, serves 12

2 T. butter, melted
8 10-inch flour tortillas
1/2 c. grated Parmesan cheese
1 egg white, beaten
Garnish: sesame, poppy and/or
    caraway seed, onion powder,
    cayenne pepper or dried cumin

Brush butter lightly over one side of each tortilla; sprinkle evenly with cheese and press down lightly. Carefully turn tortillas over. Brush other side with egg white and sprinkle with desired seeds and seasoning. Cut each tortilla into 4 strips with a pastry cutter or knife. Place strips cheese-side down on a baking sheet sprayed with non-stick vegetable spray. Bake at 400 degrees, on middle rack of oven, for about 8 to 10 minutes, until crisp and golden. Cool on a wire rack.

Seeded Tortilla Crisps

Melissa Fraser, Valencia, CA

Cinnamon Crisps

These little crispy treats are fun to make with the kids. Make plenty because they will go fast!

Makes about 2-1/2 dozen, serves 8

1/2 t. vanilla extract
1 T. hot water
1/2 t. cinnamon
3 T. sugar
4 6-inch flour tortillas, each
    cut into 8 wedges

Combine vanilla and water in a cup; blend cinnamon and sugar in a separate cup. Brush vanilla mixture over both sides of tortilla wedges; sprinkle with cinnamon-sugar. Place on a baking sheet sprayed with non-stick vegetable spray. Bake at 450 degrees for 5 minutes, until crisp.

Elizabeth Cyr, Wallingford, CT

Kielbasa Sausage Bites

Serve the sausage warm with cheese and crackers.

Makes 8 dozen, serves 24

2 lbs. Kielbasa sausage, sliced
1 T. oil
3 to 4 T. brown sugar, packed
1 T. vinegar
3 to 5 T. orange juice

In a large skillet over medium heat, fry sausage slices in oil until brown; drain half of the drippings. Add brown sugar, vinegar and orange juice. Cook over low heat for 40 minutes, stirring occasionally. Serve warm.

Mel Chencharick, Julian, PA

Veggie Mini Pizzas

Add other toppings to these little pizzas if you like, such as sliced onion or pepper.

Serves 6

6 pita rounds or flatbreads
1-1/2 c. pizza or pasta sauce
1 c. baby spinach
1 c. shredded mozzarella cheese
2 plum tomatoes, sliced

Place pita rounds on an ungreased baking sheet. Spread each with 1/4 cup sauce; top with spinach, cheese and tomato. Bake pizzas at 350 degrees for 15 to 20 minutes, or until cheese is bubbly.

Veggie Mini-Pizzas

Skillet Meatloaf

CHAPTER THREE

QUICK-TO-FIX
Main Dishes

Vegetable Quinoa Patties, Page 142   Homemade Fish Sticks, Page 118

Jill Valentine, Jackson, TN

Simply Scrumptious Frittata

This is a tasty way to use any remaining ham from Sunday dinner... try different cheeses for variety.

Serves 4

1 T. oil
1/2 c. onion, chopped
1/2 c. green pepper, chopped
1 to 2 cloves garlic, minced
4 Yukon Gold potatoes, cubed
    and cooked
3/4 c. cooked ham, cubed
8 eggs, beaten
salt and pepper to taste
3/4 c. shredded Cheddar cheese

Heat oil in a large heavy ovenproof skillet over medium heat. Add onion and green pepper; cook until tender. Add garlic; cook one more minute. Stir in potatoes and ham; cook until heated through. Reduce heat to medium-low; add eggs, salt and pepper. Cook 5 minutes or until eggs are firm on the bottom. Top eggs with cheese; bake at 350 degrees for 5 to 10 minutes, until cheese melts. Cut into wedges to serve.

Linda Diepholz, Lakeville, MN

Baked Chicken Chimichangas

I have been making these chicken chimis for years. I like that they are baked and not deep-fried...much healthier. People who don't even like Mexican food discover they love these. I make this recipe often and I even like the leftovers cold!

Serves 4 to 6

2 c. cooked chicken, chopped
    or shredded
1 c. salsa or picante sauce
2 c. shredded Cheddar cheese
4 green onions, chopped
1-1/2 t. ground cumin
1 t. dried oregano
8 8-inch flour tortillas
2 T. butter, melted
Garnish: additional shredded
    cheese, green onions, salsa

In a bowl, combine chicken, salsa or sauce, cheese, onions and seasonings. Spoon 1/3 cup of mixture down the center of each tortilla; fold opposite sides over filling. Roll up from bottom and place seam-side down on an ungreased baking sheet. Brush with melted butter. Bake, uncovered, at 400 degrees for 30 minutes or until golden, turning halfway through cooking. Garnish with additional cheese and onions; serve with salsa on the side, as desired.

Baked Chicken Chimichangas

Katherine Murnane, Plattsburgh, NY

Foil-Wrapped Baked Salmon

These packets can also be cooked on a hot grill. Delightful with a salad of fresh garden greens.

Serves 4

4 salmon fillets
1 onion, sliced
1/4 c. butter, diced
1 lemon, thinly sliced
1/4 c. brown sugar, packed

Place each fillet on a piece of aluminum foil that has been sprayed with non-stick vegetable spray. Top fillets evenly with onion slices, diced butter, lemon slices and brown sugar. Fold over aluminum foil tightly to make packets; make several holes in top of packets with a fork to allow steam to escape. Arrange packets on an ungreased baking sheet. Bake at 375 degrees for 15 to 20 minutes.

Sandra Sullivan, Aurora, CO

Beef & Snap Pea Stir-Fry

In a rush? Spice up tonight's dinner with my go-to recipe for healthy in a hurry! Substitute chicken or pork for the beef, if you like.

Makes 4 servings

1 c. brown rice, uncooked
1 lb. beef sirloin steak, thinly sliced
1 T. cornstarch
1/4 t. salt
1/4 t. pepper
2 t. canola oil
3/4 c. water
1 lb. sugar snap peas, trimmed
    and halved
1 red pepper, cut into bite-size pieces
6 green onions, thinly sliced
    diagonally, white and green
    parts divided
1 T. fresh ginger, peeled and grated
1/2 t. red pepper flakes
salt and pepper to taste
2 T. lime juice

Cook rice according to package directions. Fluff with a fork; cover and set aside. Meanwhile, sprinkle beef with cornstarch, salt and pepper; toss to coat. Heat oil in a skillet over medium-high heat. Add half of beef and brown on both sides. Transfer to a plate; repeat with remaining beef. Stir in water, peas, red pepper, white part of onions, ginger and red pepper flakes; season with salt and pepper. Cook until peas turn bright green, one to 2 minutes. Return beef to skillet; cook for another 2 to 3 minutes. Remove from heat. Stir in lime juice and green part of onions. Serve over rice.

Beef & Snap Pea Stir-Fry

Emily Selmer, Sumner, WA

Thai Peanut Noodles

If you want to purchase raw shrimp and cook and peel it yourself, start with 2 pounds. Chicken breasts are a nice substitute for shrimp.

Serves 4

1 lb. cooked, peeled medium shrimp
1 c. light Italian salad dressing, divided
2 T. crunchy peanut butter
1 T. soy sauce
1 T. honey
1 t. ground ginger
3/4 t. red pepper flakes
1 carrot, peeled and shredded
1 c. green onions, chopped
1 T. sesame oil
8-oz. pkg. angel hair pasta, cooked
2 T. fresh cilantro, chopped
Optional: 2/3 c. peanuts, chopped

Coat shrimp with 1/2 cup Italian salad dressing; refrigerate 30 minutes. Whisk together remaining 1/2 cup Italian salad dressing, peanut butter, soy sauce, honey, ginger and red pepper flakes until smooth; set aside. In a skillet, sauté carrot, green onions and shrimp in sesame oil about 5 minutes or until shrimp are thoroughly heated. Toss pasta, peanut sauce and shrimp mixture together in a large serving bowl; sprinkle with cilantro and, if desired, chopped peanuts.

J.J. Presley, Portland, TX

Cheesy Sausage-Potato Casserole

Add some fresh green beans too, if you like.

Serves 6 to 8

3 to 4 potatoes, sliced
2 8-oz. links sausage, sliced into 2-inch lengths
1 onion, chopped
1/2 c. butter, sliced
1 c. shredded Cheddar cheese

Layer potatoes, sausage and onion in a skillet sprayed with non-stick vegetable spray. Dot with butter; sprinkle with cheese. Bake at 350 degrees for 1-1/2 hours.

Cheesy Sausage-Potato Casserole

Rachel Rowden, Festus, MO

Busy Mom's Biscuit Cheeseburger Pizza

This is a go-to for my family of four on those nights we have softball and tee ball practice. My 12-year-old daughter Isabella and 6-year-old daughter Carly both love this recipe.

Makes 8 servings

1 lb. ground beef
1 T. dried minced onion
salt and pepper to taste
10-3/4 oz. can Cheddar cheese soup
16-oz. tube refrigerated biscuits
1 c. shredded Cheddar cheese
Garnish: cheeseburger condiments

Brown beef in a skillet with onion; drain and season with salt and pepper. Stir in soup; set aside. Stretch biscuits and press together to form a crust; place on a baking sheet sprayed with non-stick vegetable spray. Top crust with beef mixture; sprinkle evenly with cheese. Bake at 350 degrees for 10 minutes or until crust is golden and cheese is melted. Cut into squares; serve with your favorite condiments.

Charlie Tuggle, Palo Alto, CA

Chicken Enchilada Nacho Bowls

Your family will love this combination of hot and cold all in one bowl.

Serves 4

1 onion, diced
1 T. olive oil
10-oz. can enchilada sauce
1 c. canned crushed tomatoes
15-1/2 oz. can black beans, drained
 and rinsed
1 t. dried oregano
1 T. brown sugar, packed
2 c. rotisserie chicken, shredded
8-oz. pkg. tortilla or corn chips,
 coarsely crushed
1-1/4 c. shredded Cheddar cheese
2 c. lettuce, shredded
1/4 c. fresh cilantro, chopped
Garnish: 4 lime slices
Optional: hot pepper sauce

In a skillet over medium-high heat, sauté onion in oil until softened. Add enchilada sauce, tomatoes, beans, oregano and sugar; cook, stirring occasionally, until hot and slightly cooked down, about 5 minutes. Stir in chicken; cook until warmed through. To serve, divide chips among 4 bowls; top with chicken mixture, cheese, lettuce and cilantro. Serve with lime slices and hot sauce, if desired.

Chicken Enchilada Nacho Bowls

Carmen Chandler, Roseburg, OR

Potluck Beef Sandwiches

I tried this recipe when I was first married, almost thirty years ago. I didn't know how to cook and this one turned out well every time!

Serves 4

1 lb. ground beef
1/4 onion, chopped
salt and pepper to taste
2/3 c. barbecue sauce
2 8-oz. tubes refrigerated
   crescent rolls
1/2 to 1 c. shredded Cheddar cheese
Garnish: additional barbecue sauce

In a skillet over medium heat, brown beef and onion. Add a little salt and pepper; drain. Mix in barbecue sauce. Place crescent rolls on a baking sheet and make a rectangle, pinching seams together. Spoon beef mixture down center of dough and sprinkle with cheese. Fold the sides over and seal dough down the center. Bake at 375 degrees for 20 minutes, or until golden. Slice into portions and serve with additional barbecue sauce.

Wendi Knowles, Pittsfield, ME

Chicken Cacciatore

We love this classic chicken recipe! Make plenty of this dish because it warms up so well.

Makes 10 servings

3 lbs. chicken, skin removed if
   desired
1/4 c. all-purpose flour
1 T. olive oil
1 c. onion, thinly sliced
1/2 c. green pepper, sliced
1 clove garlic, minced
1/4 c. chicken broth
15-oz. can diced tomatoes, drained
8-oz. can tomato sauce
1/4 c. sliced mushrooms
1/4 t. dried oregano
1/8 t. salt

Pat chicken pieces dry; coat chicken with flour. In a large skillet, heat oil over medium heat. Place chicken in skillet and cook for about 15 to 20 minutes, until golden on both sides. Remove chicken to a plate; cover with aluminum foil and set aside. Add onion, green pepper and garlic to drippings in skillet; cook and stir until vegetables are tender. Add broth, scraping up brown bits in bottom of skillet. Add remaining ingredients; stir until blended. Return chicken to skillet, spooning some of the sauce over chicken. Cover and cook for about one hour, until chicken is tender and juices run clear.

Chicken Cacciatore

Nicole Wood, Ontario, Canada

Easy Pizza Peppers

This recipe is also wonderful with Cheddar cheese. Try adding olives, pineapple tidbits or your favorite pizza toppings too!

Makes 4 servings

1 lb. extra lean ground beef
1/2 c. onion, chopped
salt and pepper to taste
4 red or yellow peppers, halved
   lengthwise
4 T. water, divided
15-oz. bottle pizza sauce
Garnish: shredded mozzarella
   cheese

Brown beef with onion, salt and pepper in a skillet over medium heat: drain. Place pepper halves on 2 plates; add 2 tablespoons water to each plate. Microwave on high for 5 minutes, or until peppers are soft. Spoon beef mixture into peppers; arrange on a baking sheet. Spoon pizza sauce onto beef mixture; cover with cheese. Bake at 375 degrees for 15 minutes, or until cheese is melted.

Jen Sell, Farmington, MN

Chicken Cordon Bleu

This is a special dish I serve family & friends. It is delicious and beautiful every time.

Makes 4 servings

4 4-oz. boneless, skinless chicken
   breasts
2 slices deli ham, cut in half
2 slices Swiss cheese, cut in half
1 egg, beaten
1/2 c. milk
1/4 c. whole-grain bread crumbs
1/2 t. garlic powder
1 t. dried oregano
2 T. grated Parmesan cheese

Flatten chicken breasts between 2 pieces of wax paper until 1/4-inch thick. Top each piece with a 1/2 slice of ham and cheese; roll up tightly, securing with toothpicks. In a small bowl, beat egg and milk together; set aside. In another bowl, combine bread crumbs, garlic powder, oregano and Parmesan cheese. Dip each chicken bundle in egg mixture, then in bread crumbs. Place on a greased baking sheet; bake at 350 degrees for 45 minutes.

Chicken Cordon Bleu

Mary Thomason-Smith,
Bloomington, IN

Lemon Pepper Rainbow Trout

A favorite of my children, this recipe is fast easy, and healthy...a delicious light meal for any weeknight. Serve with a tossed salad and baked potato for a complete meal.

Serves 4

4 rainbow trout fillets
1 T. butter, melted
1 t lemon zest
2 T. lemon juice
1 T. lemon pepper seasoning

Preheat broiler on high; position oven rack on level closest to the broiler. Spray an aluminum foil-lined baking sheet lightly with non-stick vegetable spray. Arrange fish fillets on baking sheet; set aside. Combine melted butter, lemon zest and lemon juice; brush over fish. Season with lemon pepper. Broil fish on rack closest to broiler for 5 minutes, or until fish flakes easily.

Tara Horton, Delaware, OH

Chicken Pesto Primo

One summer I grew basil in my garden and froze batches of homemade pesto in ice cube trays. I made up this recipe to use that yummy pesto. When asparagus isn't in season, I'll toss in some broccoli flowerets...it's just as tasty!

Serves 4

8-oz. pkg. rotini pasta, uncooked
2 c. cooked chicken, cubed
1 c. asparagus, steamed and cut into
    1-inch pieces
2 T. basil pesto sauce
1/4 to 1/2 c. chicken broth

Cook pasta according to package directions; drain. In a skillet over medium heat, combine chicken, asparagus, pesto, cooked pasta and 1/4 cup chicken broth. Cook and stir until heated through, adding more broth as needed.

Chicken Pesto Primo

Flo Burtnett, Gage, OK

One-Pot Spaghetti

Mmm good...spaghetti from scratch, and no need to use all the pans in the kitchen. My grandson Clay eats it up!

Serves 4

1 lb. ground beef
1 onion, diced
2 14-oz. cans chicken broth
6-oz. can tomato paste
1/2 t. dried oregano
1/2 t. salt
1/4 t. pepper
1/8 t. garlic powder
8-oz. pkg. spaghetti, uncooked
   and broken
Garnish: grated Parmesan cheese

Brown ground beef and onion in a large skillet over medium heat. Drain; return to skillet. Stir in broth, tomato paste and seasonings; bring to a boil. Add spaghetti; reduce heat and simmer, stirring often, about 15 minutes or until spaghetti is tender. Sprinkle with cheese.

Linda Kilgore, Kittanning, PA

Deep-Dish Skillet Pizza

This recipe is my husband's. He made us one of these pizzas for supper and now it's the only pizza we ever want to eat. Delicious!

Serves 4

1 loaf frozen bread dough, thawed
1 to 2 15-oz. jars pizza sauce
1/2 lb. ground pork sausage, browned
   and drained
5-oz. pkg. sliced pepperoni
1/2 c. sliced mushrooms
1/2 c. green pepper, sliced
Italian seasoning to taste
1 c. shredded mozzarella cheese
1 c. shredded Cheddar cheese

Generously grease a large cast-iron skillet. Press thawed dough into the bottom and up the sides of skillet. Spread desired amount of pizza sauce over dough. Add favorite toppings, ending with cheeses on top. Bake at 425 degrees for 30 minutes. Carefully remove skillet from oven. Let stand several minutes; pizza will finish baking in the skillet. Cut into wedges to serve.

Deep-Dish Skillet Pizza

Liz Plotnick-Snay, Gooseberry Patch

My Favorite One-Pot Meal

Curry powder, raisins and chopped apple make this chicken dish just a little different.

Makes 3 to 4 servings

2 onions, diced
1/4 c. oil, divided
2-1/2 to 3 lbs. boneless,
    skinless chicken breasts
14-1/2 oz. can diced tomatoes
1/2 c. white wine or chicken broth
1 T. curry powder
1/4 t. garlic powder
1/4 t. dried thyme
1/4 t. nutmeg
1 apple, peeled, cored and cubed
1/4 c. raisins
3 T. whipping cream
1/2 t. lemon juice
2 c. cooked rice

Sauté onions in 2 tablespoons oil over medium heat in a large skillet; remove onions and set aside. Add remaining oil and chicken to skillet; cook chicken until golden. Return onions to skillet; add tomatoes, wine or broth and spices. Mix well; reduce heat, cover and simmer for 20 minutes. Add apple, raisins and cream; simmer over low heat for an additional 6 to 8 minutes. Stir in lemon juice. Serve over cooked rice.

Deb Grumbine, Greeley, CO

Deb's Garden Bounty Dinner

I love to make this dish because it is a complete meal in a skillet. My entire family loves it when I serve this for a weeknight dinner.

Makes 6 servings

1 T. oil
6 chicken drumsticks
8 zucchini, chopped
1 lb. mushrooms, chopped
1/2 green pepper, chopped
1/2 red pepper, chopped
1 onion, chopped
2 15-oz. cans stewed tomatoes
2 t. garlic, minced
1 t. turmeric
1/2 t. pepper
2 c. cooked brown rice

Heat oil in a skillet over medium-high heat. Add chicken and cook 20 to 25 minutes, or until golden. Set aside and keep warm. Add remaining ingredients except rice to skillet; cook 5 minutes. Return chicken to skillet and continue to cook until juices run clear. Serve alongside servings of rice.

Deb's Garden Bounty Dinner

Mandi Smith, Delaware, OH

Salsa Ranch Skillet

I created this delicious recipe for competition in the Ohio State Fair. It's very tasty, quick and easy to make.

Serves 4 to 6

1 lb. ground beef
1/2 c. sweet onion, chopped
1/2 c. green pepper, chopped
2.8-oz. pkg. ranch salad
   dressing mix
1 c. water
15-oz. can tomato sauce
16-oz. jar mild salsa
16-oz. can baked beans
8-oz. pkg. rotini pasta, uncooked
1 c. shredded Colby & Monterey
   Jack cheese

Brown ground beef with onion and green pepper in a large skillet over high heat. Stir in dressing mix until thoroughly blended. Stir in water, tomato sauce, salsa and beans; bring to a boil. Add pasta; reduce to medium-low heat. Simmer for 12 to 15 minutes until pasta is tender, stirring occasionally. Remove from heat; sprinkle with cheese and let stand for 5 minutes, until cheese melts and sauce thickens.

Glenna Martin, Uwchland, PA

Chicken Spaghetti

This is an old family favorite. It is a complete meal in a skillet!

Serves 4

1 lb. boneless, skinless chicken
   breasts, cut into bite-size pieces
1/4 to 1/2 c. butter
1 onion, chopped
8-oz. can sliced mushrooms, drained
16-oz. pkg. frozen broccoli flowerets,
   thawed
1 clove garlic, minced
salt and pepper to taste
16-oz. pkg. spaghetti, cooked
Garnish: grated Parmesan cheese

In a large skillet, sauté chicken in butter until no longer pink. Add onion, mushrooms, broccoli and garlic; sauté until chicken is cooked through and vegetables are tender. Add salt and pepper to taste; toss with cooked spaghetti. Sprinkle with Parmesan cheese.

Chicken Spaghetti

Jo Ann, Gooseberry Patch

Spinach-Cheddar Quiche

Try this recipe using a variety of other veggies like asparagus, mushrooms or artichokes. Great for brunch as well as dinner!

Makes 6 to 8 servings

1 loaf Italian bread, torn into bite-
  size pieces
1 onion, chopped
2 10-oz. pkgs. frozen chopped
  spinach, thawed and drained
4 c. shredded Cheddar cheese
4 eggs, beaten
1-1/2 c. milk
salt, pepper and garlic powder
  to taste
Garnish: sour cream

Combine all ingredients except sour cream; pour into a large greased skillet. Bake at 350 degrees for 40 to 50 minutes, until a knife inserted into the center comes out clean. Cut into wedges. Serve with sour cream on the side.

Shelley Turner, Boise, ID

Homemade Fish Sticks

My kids love these yummy fish sticks! I serve them in diner-style baskets with French fries.

Makes 8 servings

2 lbs. cod fillets
2 eggs
2 T. water
salt and pepper to taste
1-1/2 c. seasoned dry bread crumbs
3 T. grated Parmesan cheese
1/4 c. olive oil
1/2 c. tartar sauce
Optional: lemon wedges

Cut fish into 4-inch by one-inch strips; set aside. In a shallow dish, beat together egg, water and seasonings. In a separate dish, mix bread crumbs and cheese. Dip fish into egg mixture; coat with bread crumb mixture and set aside. Heat olive oil in a skillet over medium-high heat. Working in batches, add fish to skillet and cook until flaky and golden, about 3 minutes per side. Drain fish sticks on paper towels. Serve with tartar sauce and lemon wedges, if desired.

Homemade Fish Sticks

Cindy McKinnon, El Dorado, AR

Unstuffed Cabbage

Cabbage has very few carbs... basically you can eat all you want. So I started making this and I try to keep it around always. When I get hungry, this is my go-to food. It fills me up, and it's so good too!

Makes 12 servings

1 T. extra-virgin olive oil
1-1/2 to 2 lbs. lean ground beef
1 onion, chopped
1 clove garlic, minced
2 14-1/2 oz. cans diced tomatoes
1/2 c. water
8-oz. can tomato sauce
1 head cabbage, chopped
1 t. salt
1 t. pepper

In a large skillet, heat olive oil over medium heat; add beef and onion. Cook and stir until beef is no longer pink and onion is tender. Add garlic and continue cooking for one minute; drain. Add tomatoes with juice and remaining ingredients; stir. Cook over medium heat for 15 to 20 minutes.

Elizabeth Cisneros, Chino Hills, CA

Chicken & Sausage Skilletini

I like to make this on weeknights for a special meal together.

Serves 4 to 6

2 boneless, skinless chicken breasts, cubed
1/2 lb. spicy ground pork sausage
1 red onion, thinly sliced
2 cloves garlic, minced
14-1/2 oz. can diced tomatoes
1 red pepper, sliced
3 T. brown sugar, packed
1 t. dried basil
1/2 t. dried oregano
1/8 t. salt
1/8 t. pepper
16-oz pkg. linguine pasta, cooked
Optional: fresh oregano leaves

Heat oil in a large skillet over medium heat. Add chicken, sausage, onion and garlic; cook until juices run clear when chicken is pierced. Add tomatoes, red pepper, brown sugar, basil, oregano, salt and pepper; simmer 5 minutes. Add cooked pasta and simmer an additional 5 minutes. Garnish with oregano, if desired.

Chicken & Sausage Skilletini

Peggy Sanders, Adair, IA

Taco in a Pan

This recipe was originally given to me by my mother. It's a family favorite that's asked for time & time again. I have since passed it on to my sons.

Serves 4 to 6

1 lb. ground beef
1/2 c. onion, chopped
1/2 c. green pepper, chopped
2 c. water
1-1/4 oz. pkg. taco seasoning mix
1-1/2 c. instant rice, uncooked
1 c. salsa, or to taste
1 c. shredded Colby Jack cheese
1 tomato, chopped
Optional: 1 c. sliced black olives
Garnish: crushed nacho-flavored
    tortilla chips

Brown beef, onion and green pepper in a skillet over medium heat; drain.

Stir water and taco seasoning into beef mixture. Bring to a boil; stir in rice. Cover and cook for about 3 to 5 minutes, until rice is tender. Sprinkle salsa and cheese over all. Remove from heat; cover and let stand until cheese melts. Top with tomato and olives, if desired. Garnish with chips.

Cris Goode, Morresville, IN

Good & Healthy "Fried" Chicken

We love this healthier version of everyone's favorite food...fried chicken!

Makes 5 servings

1 c. whole-grain panko bread crumbs
1 c. cornmeal
2 T. all-purpose flour
salt and pepper to taste
1 c. buttermilk
10 chicken drumsticks

Combine panko, cornmeal, flour, salt and pepper in a gallon-size plastic zipping bag. Coat chicken with buttermilk, one piece at a time. Drop chicken into bag and shake to coat pieces lightly. Arrange chicken on a baking sheet coated with non-stick vegetable spray. Bake, uncovered, at 350 degrees for 40 to 50 minutes, until chicken juices run clear.

Good & Healthy "Fried" Chicken

Julie Swenson, Minneapolis, MN

Spicy Pork Noodle Bowls

So colorful and so tasty. We make these often.

Serves 4

8-oz. pkg. linguine pasta, uncooked
   and divided
2 T. oil, divided
1 lb. boneless pork shoulder, sliced
   into strips
1 onion, thinly sliced
1/2 lb. broccoli, cut into bite-size
   flowerets
2 T. Worcestershire sauce
1 T. soy sauce
2 t. cornstarch
1/2 t. curry powder
1 tomato, chopped

Cook half of pasta according to package directions; set aside. Reserve remaining pasta for another recipe. Heat one tablespoon oil in a large skillet over high heat. Add pork; cook and stir until golden, about 7 minutes. Remove pork; set aside. Heat remaining oil in skillet; add onion and broccoli. Cook and stir until tender, about 5 minutes. Mix together sauces, cornstarch and curry powder in a cup; stir into skillet. Cook and stir until slightly thickened. Return pork to pan; heat through. Divide cooked pasta into 4 shallow bowls. Top with pork mixture and tomato; toss to coat pasta.

Amy Butcher, Columbus, GA

Garlicky Baked Shrimp

Here's the perfect party recipe... guests peel their own shrimp and save you the work! French bread is perfect to sop up the savory sauce.

Serves 6

2 lbs. uncooked large shrimp,
   cleaned and unpeeled
16-oz. bottle Italian salad dressing
1-1/2 T. pepper
2 cloves garlic, pressed
2 lemons, halved
1/4 c. fresh parsley, chopped
1/2 c. butter, cut into pieces

Place shrimp, salad dressing, pepper and garlic in a large, oven-proof skillet, tossing to coat. Squeeze juice from lemons over shrimp mixture and stir. Cut lemon halves into wedges and add to skillet. Sprinkle shrimp with parsley; dot with butter. Bake, uncovered, at 375 degrees for about 25 minutes, stirring after 15 minutes.

Garlicky Baked Shrimp

Mary Kelly, Jefferson City, MO

Chicken & Rotini Stir-Fry

This very tasty, light recipe is so easy to make. You're gonna love it!

Serves 4 to 6

2-1/2 c. rotini pasta, uncooked
2 T. olive oil
2 boneless, skinless chicken breasts, cut into strips
1 c. broccoli flowerets
1 c. carrots, peeled and cut into curls with a vegetable peeler
1/2 c. red onion, sliced
1/4 c. water
1/2 t. chicken bouillon granules
1/2 t. fresh tarragon, snipped
2 T. grated Parmesan cheese

Cook pasta according to package directions; drain. Meanwhile, heat oil in a large skillet over medium-high heat. Add chicken, broccoli, carrots and onion. Cook and stir until broccoli is crisp-tender, about 10 minutes. Add water, bouillon and tarragon; cook and stir until juices run clear when chicken is pierced. Add pasta and cheese. Toss to coat; serve immediately.

Lynda McCormick, Burkburnett, TX

Greek Pita Pizzas

These are my healthy go-to summer pizzas. Kids and adults love them! For a crisper crust, spritz pitas with olive oil spray and a pinch of coarse salt, then broil for one to 2 minutes before adding the toppings.

Makes 8 servings

10-oz. pkg. frozen chopped spinach, thawed and well drained
4 green onions, chopped
chopped fresh dill to taste
4 whole-wheat pita rounds, split
4 roma tomatoes, sliced 1/2-inch thick
1/2 c. crumbled feta cheese with basil & tomato
dried oregano or Greek seasoning to taste

Mix spinach, onions and dill in a small bowl. Season with garlic salt and pepper; set aside. Place pita rounds on ungreased baking sheets. Arrange tomato slices among pitas. Spread spinach mixture evenly over tomatoes; spread cheese over tomatoes. Sprinkle with desired seasoning. Bake at 450 degrees for about 10 minutes.

Greek Pita Pizzas

Sharon Demers, Dolores, CO

Beef in Rosemary-Mushroom Sauce

Add some roasted redskin potatoes and a simple tossed salad for an oh-so-elegant yet easy dinner!

Serves 4

1-lb. boneless top sirloin steak, about 3/4-inch thick
8-oz. pkg. sliced mushrooms
1 c. white wine or chicken broth
10-1/2 oz. can beef broth
8-oz. can tomato sauce
1 c. green onions, chopped
1/4 c. fresh parsley, chopped and divided
1-1/2 t. fresh rosemary, chopped
1-1/2 t. balsamic vinegar
4 cloves garlic, minced

Place steak in a large plastic zipping bag; top with mushrooms and wine or broth. Refrigerate 30 minutes, turning occasionally. Remove steak from bag, reserving mushrooms and marinade. Lightly spray a large non-stick skillet with non-stick vegetable spray and place over medium-high heat. Add steak and cook 6 minutes or to desired degree of doneness, turning after 3 minutes. Remove steak from skillet; keep warm. Combine beef broth, tomato sauce, green onions, 2 tablespoons parsley and next 3 ingredients in a medium bowl. Add parsley mixture, mushrooms and marinade to skillet; bring to a boil. Cook until reduced to 2 cups, about 15 minutes, stirring frequently. Thinly slice steak diagonally across the grain and place on a serving platter. Spoon sauce over steak; sprinkle with remaining 2 tablespoons parsley.

Denise Mainville, Elk Rapids, MI

Hobo Dinner

My mom and I have made this recipe for years. It's quick, delicious and so easy the kids can help assemble it.

Serves 4 to 6

1-1/2 lbs. ground beef
1 t. Worcestershire sauce
1/2 t. seasoned pepper
1/8 t. garlic powder
3 redskin potatoes, sliced
1 onion, sliced
3 carrots, peeled and halved
olive oil and dried parsley to taste

Combine beef, Worcestershire sauce, pepper and garlic powder; form into 4 to 6 patties. Place each patty on an 18-inch length of aluminum foil. Divide slices of potato, onion and carrots evenly and place on each patty. Sprinkle with olive oil and parsley to taste. Wrap tightly in aluminum foil and arrange on a baking sheet; bake at 375 degrees for one hour.

Hobo Dinner

Pamela Chorney,
Providence Forge, VA

Chicken-Pepper Pasta

My husband and I love this dish. The aroma is wonderful!

Serves 4 to 6

6 T. margarine
1 onion, chopped
1 red pepper, chopped
1 yellow pepper, chopped
1 orange pepper, chopped
1 t. garlic, minced
3 lbs. boneless, skinless chicken
    breasts, cut into strips
1 T. fresh tarragon, minced
3/4 t. salt
1/4 t. pepper
3/4 c. half-and-half
1 c. shredded mozzarella cheese
1/2 c. grated Parmesan cheese
7-oz. pkg. vermicelli, cooked

In a skillet, melt margarine until sizzling; stir in onion, peppers and garlic. Cook over medium-high heat until peppers are crisp-tender, 2 to 3 minutes. Remove vegetables from skillet with a slotted spoon and set aside. Add chicken, tarragon, salt and pepper to skillet. Continue cooking, stirring occasionally, until chicken is golden and tender, 7 to 9 minutes. Add vegetables, half-and-half and cheeses to chicken mixture. Reduce heat to medium; continue heating until cheese has melted, about 3 to 5 minutes. Add vermicelli; toss gently to coat. Serve immediately.

Diane Cohen, Breinigsville, PA

Italian Sausage & Potato Roast

So easy...everything is baked on a sheet pan!

Makes 4 servings

3/4 lb. redskin potatoes,
    cut into quarters
1 yellow pepper, sliced into strips
1 green pepper, sliced into strips
1/2 sweet onion, sliced
1 T. olive oil
1 t. garlic salt or garlic powder
1/4 t. dried oregano
pepper to taste
1 lb. Italian pork sausage,
    cut into chunks

In a large bowl, toss vegetables with olive oil and seasonings. Line a large rimmed baking sheet with aluminum foil; lightly mist with non-stick vegetable spray. Spread vegetables on baking sheet. Place sausage chunks among vegetables. Bake, uncovered, at 450 degrees until sausage is cooked through and vegetables are tender, about 30 minutes, stirring twice during baking.

Italian Sausage & Potato Roast

Beth Bundy, Long Prairie, MN

Easy Bacon Frittata

Delicious and oh-so simple to put together! Pair with fruit salad for brunch or a crisp green salad for an easy dinner.

Makes 6 servings

3 T. oil
2 c. frozen shredded hashbrowns
7 eggs, beaten
2 T. milk
12 slices bacon, crisply cooked and crumbled
3/4 c. shredded Cheddar cheese

Heat oil in a large skillet over medium heat. Add hashbrowns and cook for 10 to 15 minutes, stirring often, until golden. In a bowl, whisk together eggs and milk. Pour egg mixture over hashbrowns in skillet; sprinkle with bacon. Cover and reduce heat to low. Cook for 10 minutes, or until eggs are set. Sprinkle with cheese; remove from heat. Cover and let stand about 5 minutes, until cheese is melted. Cut into wedges to serve.

Angela Murphy, Tempe, AZ

Mom's Homemade Pizza

Nothing is better than homemade pizza!

Makes 10 servings

8-oz. can tomato sauce
1/2 t. sugar
1/4 t. pepper
1 t. garlic powder
1-1/2 t. dried thyme
3 T. grated Parmesan cheese
1 onion, finely chopped
5 roma tomatoes, sliced
1 c. fresh spinach, chopped
1 c. shredded part-skim mozzarella cheese

Prepare Pizza Dough. Combine tomato sauce, sugar and seasonings; spread over dough. Top with Parmesan cheese, onion, tomatoes, spinach and shredded cheese. Bake at 400 degrees for 25 to 30 minutes, until edges are golden.

Pizza Dough:
1 env. quick-rise yeast
1 c. hot water
2 T. olive oil
1/2 t. salt
3 c. all-purpose flour, divided
1 T. cornmeal

Combine yeast and water. Let stand 5 minutes. Add olive oil, salt and half of the flour. Stir to combine. Stir in remaining flour. Gather into a ball and place in oiled bowl. Turn dough over and cover with plastic wrap. Let rise 30 minutes. Brush oil over a 15"x10" sheet pan or 2, 12" round pizza pans; sprinkle with cornmeal. Roll out dough; place on pan.

Mom's Homemade Pizza

Kristen Blanton, Big Bear City, CA

Dad's Cajun Dinner

Add more Cajun seasoning and hot pepper sauce if you dare!

Makes 6 servings

1 onion, diced
1 t. garlic, minced
2 T. butter
2 green peppers, diced
5 stalks celery, diced
3 T. Cajun seasoning
14-oz. pkg. Kielbasa, sliced
15-oz. can kidney beans,
    drained and rinsed
14-1/2 oz. can diced tomatoes
12-oz. can tomato juice
hot pepper sauce to taste
3 c. cooked rice

In a skillet, sauté onion and garlic in butter until onion is crisp-tender. Add peppers, celery and seasoning; continue to sauté until vegetables are tender. Add Kielbasa; sauté an additional 3 to 4 minutes. Add beans, tomatoes and tomato juice; cook until heated through. Sprinkle with hot sauce to taste. Serve over cooked rice.

Kari Hodges, Jacksonville, TX

Skillet Goulash

I like to serve up this old-fashioned family favorite with thick slices of freshly baked sweet cornbread, topped with pats of butter.

Makes 8 to 10 servings

2 lbs. ground beef
10-oz. can diced tomatoes with
    green chiles
1 lb. redskin potatoes,
    cut into quarters
15-oz. can tomato sauce
15-1/4 oz. can corn, drained
14-1/2 oz. can ranch-style beans
salt and pepper to taste
Garnish: shredded Cheddar cheese

Brown beef in a large, deep skillet over medium heat; drain. Add tomatoes with juice and remaining ingredients except garnish; reduce heat. Cover and simmer until potatoes are tender and mixture has thickened, about 45 minutes. Garnish with Cheddar cheese.

Skillet Goulash

Janet Sue Burns, Granbury, TX

Janet Sue's Crab Cakes

Lump crabmeat, whole pieces of white crabmeat, is the preferred choice for crab cakes. Serve these cakes with a squeeze of lemon or your favorite sauce to enhance the cakes' delicate flavor.

Makes 8 servings, 2 each

3 lbs. fresh crabmeat
1-1/4 c. mayonnaise
3 eggs, beaten
1/4 c. onion, minced
3/4 t. seasoned salt
1/8 t. pepper
2 T. dry mustard
3/4 c. diced pimentos, drained
1 c. green pepper, diced
1 T. Worcestershire sauce
1-1/4 c. dry bread crumbs
Optional: lemon wedges

Separate and flake the crabmeat with a fork; set aside. Combine mayonnaise and next 8 ingredients in a bowl. Add crabmeat; mix well. Fold in bread crumbs; divide into 16 portions and shape into patties. Arrange on an ungreased baking sheet and bake at 425 degrees for 10 to 15 minutes until golden. Serve with lemon wedges, if desired.

Roberta Goll, Chesterfield, MI

Roberta's Pepper Steak

This beef dish is as beautiful as it is yummy. I like to serve it right from the cast-iron skillet that I cook it in. Everyone always comments on it and wants the recipe!

Makes 8 servings

1-1/4 lbs. beef round steak, sliced
    into 1/2-inch strips
2 t. canola oil
2 cloves garlic, pressed and divided
2 green and/or red peppers, cut into
    thin strips
2 onions, coarsely chopped
8-oz. pkg. sliced mushrooms
1/2 t. salt
1/2 t. pepper
1 c. beef broth

In a skillet over medium heat, brown steak strips with oil and half the garlic. Add peppers and onions; cook until tender. Stir in mushrooms, salt, pepper and remaining garlic. Stir in beef broth. Reduce heat to low and simmer for one hour. Add a little water if needed.

Roberta's Pepper Steak

Andrea Heyart, Savannah, TX

Cozy Potato Burritos

I love this hearty recipe in the fall. It's warm and spicy...the potato really makes it stick to your ribs. Or slice these burritos pinwheel-style and serve them as tasty appetizers.

Makes 10 servings

1 lb. ground beef
1 russet potato, peeled and shredded
3 green onions, diced, both green
    and white parts
15-oz. can diced tomatoes, drained
4-oz. can diced green chiles
1 T. garlic, minced
salt and pepper to taste
10 10-inch flour tortillas
16-oz. pkg. shredded Cheddar cheese
Optional: 1/4 c. fresh cilantro,
    chopped
Garnish: sour cream

Brown beef in a large skillet over medium heat. Drain; add potato, onions, tomatoes, chiles, garlic, salt and pepper. Cook over medium heat for about 15 minutes, stirring often, until potato is soft and tender. Remove from heat. For each burrito, cover one tortilla with cheese; spoon some of beef mixture down the center. Top with cilantro, if desired. Roll up tightly; repeat with remaining ingredients. Serve with a dollop of sour cream on top.

Katie Majeske, Denver, CO

Prosciutto, Brie & Apple Panini

Great in chilly weather with a cup of creamy tomato soup.

Makes 2 servings

1/4 c. butter, softened
1 green onion, finely chopped
1/2 t. lemon juice
1/4 t. Dijon mustard
4 slices sourdough bread
3/4 lb. prosciutto or deli ham, thinly
    sliced
1/2 lb. brie cheese, cut into
    4 pieces and rind removed
1 Granny Smith apple, peeled, cored
    and thinly sliced

In a bowl, beat butter until creamy. Stir in onion, lemon juice and mustard until smooth. Spread half the butter mixture on one side of 2 bread slices. Place slices butter-side down in a cast-iron skillet over medium heat. Top with prosciutto or ham, cheese, apple and remaining bread. Spread remaining butter on top slice. Weight sandwich with a smaller skillet or a bacon press, if desired. Cook over medium heat until bread is toasted and cheese is melted. Serve immediately.

Prosciutto, Brie & Apple Panini

Amy Butcher, Columbus, GA

Orange-Pork Stir-Fry

Short on time? Pick up a package of pork that's precut in strips just for stir-frying.

Makes 4 servings

1-oz. pkg. Italian salad dressing mix
1/4 c. orange juice
1/4 c. oil
2 T. soy sauce
1 lb. pork loin, cut into strips
16-oz. pkg. frozen Oriental vegetable blend, thawed
2-1/2 c. cooked rice

Mix together dressing mix, juice, oil and soy sauce. Combine one tablespoon of dressing mixture and pork strips in a large skillet over medium heat. Cook and stir for 4 to 5 minutes or until pork is no longer pink. Add vegetables and remaining dressing mixture; cook and stir until vegetables are crisp-tender. Serve over cooked rice.

Jo Ann, Gooseberry Patch

Picture-Perfect Paella

This classic Spanish dish is not only beautiful to look at, it's also amazingly delicious. It takes a little time to prepare, but it's so worth it.

Serves 8

3 lbs. chicken
2 onions, quartered
1 stalk celery, sliced
2 carrots, peeled and sliced
salt and pepper to taste
6 c. water
2 c. long-cooking rice, uncooked
2 cloves garlic, crushed
1/4 c. oil
1 c. peas
1/4 c. diced pimentos, drained
1/2 t. dried oregano
1/8 t. saffron or turmeric
1 lb. uncooked large shrimp, peeled and cleaned
12 uncooked clams in shells

In a large skillet over medium heat, combine chicken pieces, onions, celery, carrots, salt, pepper and water. Bring to a boil; reduce heat, cover and simmer for one hour. Remove vegetables and chicken, reserving 6 cups broth. Dice chicken and set meat aside, discarding bones. In the same skillet over medium heat, cook and stir rice and garlic in oil until golden. Add reserved chicken, reserved broth, peas, pimentos, oregano and saffron or turmeric. Cover and cook over low heat for 15 minutes. Add shrimp and clams; cover and cook for another 10 minutes, or until shrimp are pink and clams have opened.

Picture-Perfect Paella

Irene Robinson, Cincinnati, OH

Turkey Thyme Tetrazzini

A great way to use leftover roast turkey or chicken!

Serves 4

3/4 c. medium egg noodles, uncooked
1 T. butter
2 c. sliced mushrooms
1/4 c. light cream cheese spread
1 c. chicken broth
Optional: 1/4 c. fresh thyme,
    chopped, or 1 t. dried thyme
3 c. cooked turkey, cubed
1 c. frozen peas, thawed

Cook noodles according to package directions; drain. Meanwhile, melt butter in a large skillet over medium heat. Add mushrooms; cook until tender. Stir in cream cheese, broth and thyme, if using; bring to a boil. Reduce heat to low. Simmer for 7 minutes, stirring occasionally, or until slightly thickened. Add turkey and peas; cook until heated through. To serve, spoon turkey mixture over noodles.

Evelyn Moriarty, Philadelphia, PA

Vegetable Quinoa Patties

This recipe is my own, adapted from one I found online and tweaked. It has become a family favorite, especially in summertime when fresh-picked veggies are available.

Makes 6 servings

3 eggs
1/2 c. shredded part-skim
    mozzarella cheese
1/2 c. low-fat cottage cheese
1/4 c. whole-wheat flour
1 carrot, peeled and grated
1 zucchini, grated
3 T. green, red or yellow pepper,
    grated
3 green onions, finely chopped
1/2 t. ground cumin
1/4 t. garlic powder
1/8 t. salt
1/4 t. pepper
2 c. cooked quinoa
1 T. olive oil

Beat eggs in a large bowl; stir in cheeses and flour, blending well. Mix in vegetables. Combine seasonings; sprinkle over vegetable mixture and mix well. Add cooked quinoa; stir together well. Heat olive oil in a skillet over medium heat. With a small ladle, drop mixture into skillet, making 6 patties. Flatten lightly with ladle to about 1/4-inch thick. Fry patties for 4 to 5 minutes per side, until golden. Serve each serving with 3 tablespoons Dilled Yogurt Dressing.

Dilled Yogurt Dressing:
1/2 c. plain Greek yogurt
1 cucumber, peeled and diced
3 sprigs fresh dill, snipped,
    or 1/2 t. dill weed

Stir together all ingredients in a small bowl.

Vegetable Quinoa Patties

Virginia Watson, Scranton, PA

Spicy Pork Packets

Sometimes I replace the plain corn with a can of sweet corn & diced peppers to add a bit of extra color.

Serves 4

14-1/2 oz. can chicken broth
2 c. instant rice, uncooked
1-1/2 T. spicy taco mix, divided
1/8 t. cayenne pepper
1/8 t. salt
1/8 t. pepper
15-oz. can corn, drained
1/3 c. green onion, sliced
4 boneless pork chops

Heat broth to boiling in a medium saucepan; remove from heat. Add rice, one teaspoon taco mix, cayenne pepper, salt and pepper to taste. Cover and let stand for about 5 minutes until liquid is absorbed. Add corn and green onion; set aside. Sprinkle pork chops with remaining taco mix; place each on an 18-inch length of aluminum foil sprayed with non-stick cooking spray. Divide rice mixture evenly over pork chops; fold aluminum foil over to enclose food and seal tightly. Place packets on a baking sheet; cut an **X** to vent foil. Bake at 400 degrees for 45 minutes.

Lauren Vanden Berg, Grandville MI

Skillet Meatloaf

My great-grandma was very poor and only owned one cast-iron skillet. She made this meatloaf in the skillet. She passed her skillet on to my grandma, who passed it on to me. Now this is the only kind of meatloaf I make.

Serves 3 to 4

1 lb. ground beef
1 onion, chopped
1 green pepper, chopped
4 saltine crackers, crushed
1-oz. pkg. ranch salad dressing mix
1 egg
1/4 c. barbecue sauce

In a bowl, combine beef, onion and green pepper; mix well. Add cracker crumbs and dressing mix; mix again. Shape beef mixture into ball; make a little hole in the middle. Crack the egg into the hole; mix again. Preheat a cast-iron skillet or 3 to 4 individual skillets over medium heat. Shape meatloaf to fit in skillet(s). Add meatloaf to skillet(s). Spread barbecue sauce on top. Cover and cook for 30 to 35 minutes for a large skillet and 20 to 25 minutes for smaller skillets, until meatloaf is no longer pink in the center. Reduce heat to low, if needed. Use a meat thermometer to check temperature if desired.

Skillet Meatloaf

Sarah Oravecz, Gooseberry Patch

Bratwurst Pretzel Reubens

We love these sandwiches...fun for an Oktoberfest cookout! Sometimes I'll use my own home-baked soft pretzels, but I've found soft pretzels from the grocery's freezer section are good too.

Makes 4 servings

4 bratwursts, halved lengthwise
4 large soft pretzels, warmed
   if frozen
spicy brown mustard to taste
4 T. butter, divided
4 T. olive oil, divided
8 to 16 slices Muenster cheese
1 c. sauerkraut, well drained
pepper to taste

Grill or pan-fry bratwursts as desired; set aside. Meanwhile, slice pretzels in half horizontally; spread the cut sides with mustard. Working in batches, melt one tablespoon butter with one tablespoon olive oil in a skillet over medium-low heat. Add 2 pretzel halves to skillet, crust-side down. Arrange one to 2 cheese slices on each half. Cook just until cheese is nearly melted. With a spatula, remove pretzel halves to a plate. Top one pretzel half with a bratwurst; spoon on 1/4 cup sauerkraut. Season with pepper. Add pretzel top. Repeat with remaining ingredients.

Kathy Majeske, Denver, PA

Scott's Ham & Pear Sandwiches

The spiced butter makes these sweet & savory sandwiches especially crispy and good!

Makes 4 sandwiches

8 slices sourdough bread
4 slices Swiss cheese
3/4 lb. sliced deli ham
15-oz. can pear halves, drained and
   thinly sliced

Spread each slice of bread thinly with Spiced Butter spread. On each of 4 slices, place one slice of cheese; layer evenly with ham and pears. Top with remaining bread slices and press together gently. Spread outsides of sandwiches with Spiced Butter. Heat a cast-iron skillet over medium-high heat. Add sandwiches; cook until crisp and golden, about 5 minutes on each side.

Spiced Butter:
1/2 c. butter, softened
1 t. pumpkin pie spice
1/2 t. ground coriander
1/2 t. ground ginger
1/2 t. salt

Combine all ingredients until smooth and well blended. Keep refrigerated.

Scott's Ham & Pear Sandwiches

Becky Kuchenbecker, Ravenna, OH

Shortcut Stromboli

I have made this stromboli for family get-togethers, picnics and potlucks, and I've gotten many requests for this quick & easy recipe! You can use different meats and cheeses for a new taste every time.

Serves 6

1 loaf frozen bread dough, thawed
1 T. grated Parmesan cheese
2 eggs, separated
2 T. oil
1 t. dried parsley
1 t. dried oregano
1/2 t. garlic powder
1/2 lb. deli ham, sliced
1/4 lb. deli salami, sliced
6-oz. pkg. shredded Cheddar cheese

Spread thawed dough in a rectangle on a greased baking sheet. Mix Parmesan cheese, egg yolks, oil and seasonings in a bowl. Spread Parmesan cheese mixture on top of dough. Layer with meat and Cheddar cheese. Roll up jelly-roll style; place seam-side down on baking sheet. Let rise about 20 minutes. Brush with egg whites. Bake, uncovered, at 350 degrees for 30 to 40 minutes, until golden. Slice to serve.

Audrey Lett, Newark, DE

Suzanne's Tomato Melt

I love this as a quick breakfast with a cup of coffee...it is so easy to make!

Makes one serving

1 onion bagel or English muffin, split
1/4 c. shredded Cheddar cheese
2 tomato slices
1 T. grated Parmesan cheese
several fresh basil leaves

Place bagel or English muffin halves on a baking sheet, cut-sides up. Sprinkle each with half of the Cheddar cheese. Top with a tomato slice. Sprinkle half the Parmesan cheese over each tomato. Add fresh basil leaf on top. Broil about 6 inches from heat for 4 to 5 minutes, or until cheese is bubbly.

Suzanne's Tomato Melt

Jo Ann Belovitch, Stratford, CT

Seafood Dish Delight

A delicious and elegant dish that's
a snap to make. Use half shrimp and
half scallops, if you like...dress it up
with curly cavatappi pasta.

Makes 4 to 6 servings

16-oz. pkg. rotini pasta, uncooked
6 T. butter
1 bunch green onions, chopped
2 t. shrimp or seafood seasoning
1/4 t. salt
1/4 t. pepper
1/8 t. garlic powder
1 lb. fresh shrimp or scallops,
   cleaned
1 c. whipping cream

Cook pasta according to package
directions; drain and transfer to a
serving bowl. Meanwhile, melt butter
in a skillet over medium heat. Add
green onions and seasonings; cook
until tender. Add shrimp or scallops
and a little more shrimp seasoning
to taste. Cook until seafood is opaque.
Reduce heat to low; stir in cream and
heat through. Add to cooked pasta
and stir. Serve hot.

Kerry Mayer, Dunham Springs, LA

Western Pork Chops

For a delicious variation, try
substituting peeled, cubed
sweet potatoes for the redskins.

Serves 4

1 T. all-purpose flour
1 c. barbecue sauce
4 pork chops
salt and pepper to taste
4 redskin potatoes, sliced
1 green pepper, cubed
1 c. baby carrots

Shake flour in a large, plastic zipping
bag. Add barbecue sauce to bag
and squeeze bag to blend in flour.
Season pork chops with salt and
pepper; add pork chops to bag. Turn
bag to coat pork chops with sauce. On
a baking sheet, arrange vegetables
in an even layer. Remove pork
chops from bag and place on top of
vegetables. Cover with foil making
a slit on the top. Bake at 350 degrees
for about 40 to 45 minutes, until pork
chops and vegetables are tender.

Western Pork Chops

Doris Stegner, Delaware, OH

Sunday Meatball Skillet

You'll love making this meatball dinner. It goes together quickly and your family will think you worked all day making it!

Serves 4

3/4 lb. ground beef
1 c. onion, grated
1/2 c. Italian-flavored dry
   bread crumbs
1 egg, beaten
1/4 c. catsup
1/4 t. pepper
2 c. beef broth
1/4 c. all-purpose flour
1/2 c. sour cream
8-oz. pkg. medium egg noodles,
   cooked
Garnish: chopped fresh parsley

In a bowl, combine beef, onion, bread crumbs, egg, catsup and pepper. Shape into one-inch meatballs. Spray a skillet with non-stick vegetable spray. Cook meatballs over medium heat, turning occasionally, until browned, about 10 minutes. Remove meatballs and let drain on paper towels. In a bowl, whisk together broth and flour; add to skillet. Cook and stir until mixture thickens,

about 5 minutes. Stir in sour cream. Add meatballs and noodles; toss to coat. Cook and stir until heated through, about 5 minutes. Garnish with parsley.

Jennifer Catterino, Pasadena, MD

Simple Sloppy Joes

These sandwiches will be a winner with the family for their flavor and with Mom for their ease!

Serves 6 to 8

1 lb. ground beef
1 onion, chopped
1 c. catsup
1/4 c. water
2 T. Worcestershire sauce
1/4 t. salt
1/4 t. pepper
6 to 8 sandwich buns, split
dill pickle slices

Cook ground beef and onion in a large skillet over medium-high heat, stirring until beef crumbles and is no longer pink; drain. Stir in catsup, water, Worcestershire sauce, salt and pepper; simmer 20 minutes, stirring frequently. Spoon onto buns; top with dill pickle slices.

Simple Sloppy Joes

Kathy Wood, La Crescenta, CA

Oven-Baked Chicken Fingers

If busy kids can't get home for dinner, take it to them. Pack a tailgating basket and enjoy picnicking with them at the ball park. Be sure to pack extra for hungry team members!

Serves 6

1 c. Italian-flavored dry bread
   crumbs
2 T. grated Parmesan cheese
1 clove garlic, minced
1/4 c. oil
6 boneless, skinless chicken breasts

Preheat oven to 425 degrees. Heat a large baking sheet in the oven for 5 minutes. Combine bread crumbs and cheese in a shallow dish; set aside. Combine garlic and oil in a small bowl; set aside. Place chicken between 2 sheets of heavy-duty plastic wrap. Flatten chicken to 1/2-inch thickness, using a meat mallet or rolling pin; cut into one-inch-wide strips. Dip strips in oil mixture; coat with crumb mixture. Coat preheated baking sheet with non-stick vegetable spray and place chicken on prepared baking sheet. Bake chicken at 425 degrees for 12 to 14 minutes, turning after 10 minutes.

Arleena Connor, Leopold, IN

Toasted Ham & Cheese

Serve these buttery sandwiches with a side of potato chips and a crisp dill pickle, or a cup of tomato bisque... pure comfort!

Serves 4

2-1/2 T. butter, softened
8 slices sourdough bread
4 slices Colby cheese
1/2 lb. shaved deli ham
4 slices Swiss cheese

Spread butter on one side of each slice of bread. Arrange 4 bread slices, buttered-side down, in a cast-iron skillet over medium-high heat. Top with one slice Colby cheese, desired amount of ham and one slice Swiss cheese. Add remaining bread slices, buttered-side up. Grill sandwiches on both sides until golden and cheese melts.

Toasted Ham & Cheese

Rick Schulte, Wyandotte, MI

Crazy Comforting Spaghetti

This was by far the quickest and most comforting meal my wife Tiffani knew how to get onto a plate, and she always had the ingredients on hand to make it. My son Sam and I could eat it every day of the week. Tiffani passed away in 2016 at a far-too-young age. This recipe is shared in her memory.

Makes 6 to 8 servings

1 onion, chopped
1 T. butter
1 T. oil
2 cloves garlic, minced
1-1/2 lbs. ground beef
4 14-oz. cans spaghetti in tomato
    sauce & cheese
1 to 2 T. Worcestershire sauce
1 t. salt
1/2 t. pepper
Garnish: grated Parmesan cheese
Optional: hot pepper sauce

In a skillet over medium heat, cook onion in butter and olive oil until translucent. Add garlic; cook and stir for one minute more. Add beef; cook until no longer pink. Drain; add spaghetti in sauce, Worcestershire sauce and seasonings. Heat through. Serve with Parmesan cheese and hot sauce, if desired.

Carol Hickman, Kingsport, TN

Salmon Patties

A delicious standby...so quick to fix, and most of the ingredients are right in the pantry.

Makes 6 servings

15-1/2 oz. can salmon, drained
    and flaked
1/4 c. whole-wheat crackers, crushed
1/2 T. dried parsley
1/2 t. lemon zest
1 T. lemon juice
2 green onions, sliced
1 egg plus 1 egg white, beaten
1 T. canola oil

Combine all ingredients except oil; form into 6 patties. Heat oil in a skillet over medium heat. Cook patties 4 to 5 minutes on each side, until golden. Serve with one tablespoon Cucumber Sauce per serving.

Cucumber Sauce:
1/3 c. cucumber, chopped
3 T. plain yogurt
2 T. mayonnaise
1/4 t. dried tarragon

Combine all ingredients; chill until ready to serve.

Salmon Patties

Wendy Meadows, Spring Hill, FL

Scrambled Cheeseburgers

I've been making this recipe since my kids were little. They did not like traditional hamburgers and this was more to their liking. Now it's a staple on our menu. My son will actually call me to find out what night I am making this so he can come to dinner.

Makes 4 to 6 servings

1 lb. ground beef
1/2 to 3/4 c. onion, diced
Optional: garlic powder, salt and
    pepper to taste
4 slices American, Cheddar,
    Pepper Jack or Swiss cheese
4 to 6 hamburger buns, split
Garnish: favorite cheeseburger
    toppings

Add onion to a large skillet over medium heat; crumble in beef. Cook and stir, breaking up any larger pieces, until onion is translucent and beef is no longer pink. Drain. Stir in garlic powder, salt and pepper, if using. Spread beef mixture into an even layer in skillet. Arrange cheese slices over beef. Once the cheese starts to melt, stir it into the beef. Serve spooned onto buns; garnish with your favorite toppings.

Linda Strausburg, Arroyo Grande, CA

Bacon-Wrapped Chicken

Each chicken breast is coated with herb-flavored cream cheese, rolled up and wrapped in bacon, making this dish an excellent choice for special get-togethers.

Serves 2

2 boneless, skinless chicken breasts,
    flattened to 1/2-inch thickness
1/2 t. salt
1/4 t. pepper
2 T. chive-and-onion-flavored cream
    cheese, softened and divided
2 T. chilled butter, divided
1/2 t. dried tarragon, divided
2 slices bacon

Sprinkle chicken with salt and pepper. Spread one tablespoon cream cheese over each chicken breast; top with one tablespoon butter and 1/4 teaspoon tarragon. Roll up and wrap with one slice bacon; secure with a toothpick. Place chicken seam-side down on an ungreased baking sheet. Bake at 400 degrees for 30 minutes or until juices run clear when chicken is pierced with a fork. Increase temperature to broil. Watching the broiler carefully, broil 8 to 10 minutes or just until bacon is crisp.

Bacon-Wrapped Chicken

Kathy Grashoff, Fort Wayne, IN

Shrimp Creole

If your family likes Spanish Rice, they'll love this delicious seafood variation.

Serves 6 to 8

1 c. onion, chopped
1 c. green pepper, chopped
1 c. celery, sliced
2 cloves garlic, minced
1/4 c. butter
1/4 c. all-purpose flour
1 t. salt
pepper to taste
1 bay leaf
16-oz. can diced tomatoes
1-1/2 lbs. shrimp, peeled
    and cleaned
3 to 4 c. cooked rice

Sauté onion, green pepper, celery and garlic in butter in a skillet over medium heat until tender. Blend in flour; stir until golden. Add salt, pepper and bay leaf; stir in tomatoes until thick. Reduce heat to low; add shrimp and simmer, covered, for 10 minutes until shrimp are just pink, stirring occasionally. Discard bay leaf; serve over cooked rice.

Cecilia Ollivares, Santa Paula, CA

Curried Chicken with Mango

I love dishes like this one that don't take too long to make and have a unique flavor. This recipe is delicious and speedy...perfect served with a side of naan flatbread.

Serves 4 to 6

2 T. oil
4 boneless, skinless chicken breasts,
    cooked and sliced
13.6-oz. can coconut milk
1 c. mango, peeled, pitted and cubed
2 to 3 T. curry powder
cooked jasmine rice

Heat oil in a large skillet over medium heat. Cook chicken in oil until golden and warmed through. Stir in milk, mango and curry powder. Simmer for 10 minutes, stirring occasionally, or until slightly thickened. Serve over cooked rice.

Curried Chicken with Mango

Lou Miller, Savannah, MO

Skillet Macaroni & Beef

This is my favorite recipe...I usually have all the ingredients on hand and my guests always love its hearty flavor.

Serves 6 to 8

1-1/2 lbs. ground beef
2 c. elbow macaroni, uncooked
1/2 c. onion, minced
1/2 c. green pepper, chopped
2 8-oz. cans tomato sauce
1 c. water
1 T. Worcestershire sauce
1 t. salt
1/4 t. pepper

Lightly brown beef in a skillet; drain. Stir in macaroni, onion and green pepper; cook until onion is soft. Add remaining ingredients. Lower heat; cover and simmer 25 minutes or until macaroni is tender, stirring occasionally.

Jo Ann, Gooseberry Patch

Speedy Steak & Veggies

This recipe makes a complete meal and everyone thinks it is so special!

Serves 4 to 6

juice of 1 lime
salt and pepper to taste
1-1/2 lb. beef flank steak
1/2 bunch broccoli, cut into
    flowerets
2 c. baby carrots, sliced
2 ears corn, husked and cut into
    2-inch pieces
1 red onion, sliced into wedges
2 T. olive oil

Combine lime juice, salt and pepper; brush over both sides of beef. Place on a broiler pan and broil, 5 minutes per side, turning once. Set aside on a cutting board; keep warm. Toss broccoli, carrots, corn and onion with oil. Spoon onto a lightly greased baking sheet in a single layer. Bake at 475 degrees, turning once, until tender, about 10 minutes. Slice the steak into thin strips on the diagonal and arrange on a platter. Surround with vegetables.

Speedy Steak & Veggies

Gram's Zucchini in a Pan

CHAPTER FOUR

SIMPLY SATISFYING
Salads
& Sides

Green Bean Bundles, Page 188

Arugula Potato Cornugula, Page 184

Kathy Farrell, Rochester, NY

Versatile Zucchini Patties

This is a great way to get your kids to try zucchini! I have made this recipe so many times, I don't need to look at my recipe card anymore. We love it as a side dish. We even eat these patties on rolls with pasta sauce and mozzarella for a great zucchini sandwich. Or layer them like eggplant in a casserole dish to make a tasty zucchini patty Parmesan. Yum!

Serves 4 to 6

2 to 4 zucchini
2 eggs
1/2 c. all-purpose flour
1/2 c. Italian-seasoned dry
   bread crumbs
2 T. grated Parmesan cheese
1/2 t. Italian seasoning
1/4 c. olive oil
salt and pepper to taste
Optional: pasta sauce or sour cream

Shred zucchini using the larger holes of a grater; set aside. In a large bowl, beat eggs well. Add zucchini, flour, bread crumbs, Parmesan cheese and seasonings. Mix well and let stand for 20 minutes. Heat a skillet over medium heat; add olive oil. Add zucchini mixture by tablespoonfuls; flatten each slightly with a fork. Cook patties on both sides until golden. Remove to a plate lined with paper towels; drain. Serve warm, garnished with pasta sauce or sour cream, if desired.

Jennifer Niemi, Nova Scotia, Canada

Rosemary Peppers & Fusilli

This colorful, flavorful meatless meal is ready to serve in a jiffy. If you can't find fusilli pasta, try medium shells, rotini or even wagon wheels.

Makes 4 servings

2 to 4 T. olive oil
2 red onions, thinly sliced and
   separated into rings
3 red, orange and/or yellow peppers,
   very thinly sliced
5 to 6 cloves garlic, very thinly sliced
3 t. dried rosemary
salt and pepper to taste
12-oz. pkg. fusilli pasta, cooked
Optional: shredded mozzarella
   cheese

Add oil to a large skillet over medium heat. Add onions to skillet; cover and cook over medium heat for 10 minutes. Stir in remaining ingredients except pasta and cheese; reduce heat. Cook, covered, stirring occasionally, for an additional 20 minutes. Serve vegetable mixture over pasta, topped with cheese if desired.

Rosemary Peppers & Fusilli

Ann Mathis, Biscoe, AR

Lemon-Garlic Brussels Sprouts

These Brussels sprouts are so pretty because they keep their color when they are cooked this way.

Makes 6 servings

3 T. olive oil
2 lbs. Brussels sprouts, trimmed
    and halved
3 cloves garlic, minced
zest and juice of 1 lemon
sea salt and pepper to taste
3 T. Gruyère cheese, grated

Heat oil in a large skillet over medium-high heat. Add Brussels sprouts; sauté for 7 to 8 minutes. Turn sprouts over; sprinkle with garlic. Continue cooking 7 to 8 minutes, until sprouts are golden, caramelized and tender. Reduce heat to low. Add remaining ingredients except cheese; stir to combine. Adjust seasonings, if needed. Top with cheese just before serving.

Joanne Nagle, Ashtabula, OH

Country-Style Skillet Apples

A perfect partner for roast pork at dinner...for grilled breakfast sausages too!

Makes 4 to 6 servings

1/3 c. butter
1/2 c. sugar
1/2 t. cinnamon
2 T. cornstarch
1 c. water
4 Golden Delicious apples, peeled,
    cored and sliced

Melt butter in a skillet over medium heat. Stir in sugar, cinnamon and cornstarch; mix well and stir in water. Add apple slices. Cook over medium heat, stirring occasionally, until tender, about 10 minutes.

Jill Ross, Pickerington, OH

Kale & Potato Casserole

Warm potatoes, wilted greens and Parmesan cheese make this a hearty side!

Serves 4 to 6

1/4 c. butter, melted
3 potatoes, thinly sliced
10 leaves fresh kale, finely chopped
5 T. grated Parmesan cheese
salt and pepper to taste

Drizzle melted butter over potatoes in a bowl; mix well. In a greased cast-iron skillet layer 1/3 each of potatoes, kale and Parmesan cheese; season with s alt and pepper. Continue layering and seasoning, ending with cheese. Cover skillet and transfer to oven. Bake at 375 degrees for 30 minutes. Uncover; bake for another 15 to 30 minutes, until potatoes are tender.

Kale & Potato Casserole

Allene Whalen, Salinas, CA

Spicy Taco Salad

For a party presentation, arrange tortilla chips on a platter and top with ground beef and vegetables arranged in rings. Spoon the avocado sauce mixture over all.

Serves 4

1 lb. ground beef
1 head lettuce, shredded
15-1/2 oz. can kidney beans, drained
   and rinsed
6-oz. can sliced black olives, drained
3 tomatoes, sliced
4 green onions, chopped
1 c. shredded Monterey Jack cheese
2 avocados, peeled, pitted and
   mashed
1/4 c. oil
1 c. sour cream
1 T. chili powder
2 T. lemon juice
1 T. sugar
salt to taste
1/8 t. hot pepper sauce
10-oz. pkg. tortilla chips

Cook ground beef in a skillet on medium high heat until browned; drain and let cool. Toss together beef, lettuce, beans, olives, tomatoes, onions and cheese; set aside. Combine remaining ingredients except tortilla chips; toss with ground beef mixture. Add chips; toss lightly and serve immediately.

Geneva Rogers, Gillette, WY

Roasted Root Vegetables

Roasting brings out the natural sweetness of these beautiful veggies.

Makes 8 servings

4 turnips, peeled and quartered
2 parsnips, peeled and cut into
   one-inch slices
2 carrots, peeled and thickly sliced
1 yam, peeled and cut into
   one-inch slices
16 pearl onions, peeled
4 beets, peeled and quartered
4 cloves garlic
3 T. olive oil
2 T. fresh rosemary, chopped
1/4 t. pepper

Place all of the ingredients in a large plastic zipping bag. Close bag; turn several times to coat vegetables evenly. Spread mixture in a roasting pan; bake at 450 degrees for one hour.

Roasted Root Vegetables

Lisa Ann Panzino DiNunzio,
Vineland, NJ

Roasted Cauliflower with Parmesan

A simply delicious side dish that's sure to disappear quickly!

Makes 4 to 6 servings

**1 head cauliflower, cut into 1-inch
  flowerets
3 to 4 T. extra virgin olive oil
1/2 c. Italian-flavored dry
  bread crumbs
1/4 c. grated Parmesan cheese
garlic powder, salt and pepper
  to taste**

In a bowl, toss cauliflower with olive oil, bread crumbs and cheese. Spread in a single layer on a rimmed baking sheet coated with non-stick vegetable spray. Season with garlic powder, salt and pepper. Bake at 400 degrees for 25 to 35 minutes, until golden.

Melinda Daniels, Lewiston, ID

Melinda's Veggie Stir-Fry

I really like stir-fry and chow mein, so I created this recipe using the items that I had in my garden and fridge. It is now one of my family's favorites and makes great leftovers.

Serves 8

**8-oz. pkg. spaghetti, uncooked
2 c. broccoli, cut into bite-size
  flowerets
1 c. snow or sugar snap pea pods,
  halved
2 carrots, peeled and thinly sliced
1/2 onion, thinly sliced
1/4 green pepper, thinly sliced**

Cook spaghetti as package directs; drain and set aside. Meanwhile, place vegetables into a steamer basket; place in a large stockpot filled with enough water to just reach the bottom of the basket. Cook over medium heat and steam for about 3 to 5 minutes, until just beginning to soften; drain. If crisper vegetables are desired, omit this step. When spaghetti and vegetables are done, add to Stir-Fry Sauce in skillet. Cook and stir over medium-high heat for about 15 minutes, to desired tenderness.

Stir-Fry Sauce:
**1/2 c. olive oil
1/3 c. low-sodium soy sauce
2 T. Dijon mustard
2 T. sliced pepperoncini, chopped
2 cloves garlic, minced
1 t. pepper**

In a large skillet over low heat, mix all ingredients together. Simmer until sauce is heated through.

Melinda's Veggie Stir-Fry

Jen Stout, Blandon, PA

Spicy Roasted Potatoes

These potatoes are my family's favorite side dish!

Makes 4 servings

2 baking potatoes, cut into
   1-inch cubes
1-1/2 t. dry mustard
1-1/2 t. Dijon mustard
1 t. olive oil
1 clove garlic, minced
1 t. dried tarragon
1/4 t. paprika
1/8 t. cayenne pepper

Place cubed potatoes in a bowl; set aside. In a separate bowl, combine remaining ingredients; stir well and pour over potatoes. Toss potatoes until well coated. Arrange potatoes in a single layer on a lightly greased baking sheet. Bake, uncovered, at 425 degrees for 30 to 35 minutes, until tender and golden.

Diane Holland, Galena, IL

Rose's 3-Bean Dish

Everyone loves these beans and asks for the recipe. It was given to me by my sister-in-law many years ago. Add a pound of browned hamburger to this if you like.

Makes 10 servings

1/2 lb. bacon
1-1/2 c. onions, diced
1/2 c. brown sugar, packed
1 T. dry mustard
1/2 t. garlic powder
1/2 t. salt
2 16-oz. cans butter beans, drained
16-oz. can Boston baked beans,
   drained
14-1/2 oz. can lima beans, drained

In a large skillet over medium heat, cook bacon until crisp. Remove bacon to paper towels; partially drain skillet. Add onions to drippings in skillet; cook until lightly golden. Remove onions with a slotted spoon. Add brown sugar and seasonings to skillet; cook and stir until brown sugar dissolves. Return onions and crumbled bacon to skillet; add beans. Stir well and heat through over medium-low heat.

Rose's 3-Bean Dish

Jasmine Burgess, DeWitt, MI

Roasted Broccolini & Asparagus

I like to serve this fresh vegetable dish in the summer with grilled salmon for a light yet satisfying meal.

Serves 4 to 6

1-1/2 T. garlic-flavored or plain
   extra virgin olive oil
1/2 t. garlic-herb seasoning blend
1/4 t. salt
1 bunch asparagus, trimmed
1 bunch broccolini, trimmed and
   split
1/2 c. green onions, sliced
Garnish: shredded Parmesan
   cheese to taste

Combine oil and seasonings in a deep bowl. Add vegetables; toss to coat. Spread evenly onto a parchment paper-lined baking sheet. Bake at 350 degrees for 25 minutes. Remove from oven; sprinkle with cheese. Serve immediately.

Tena Huckleby, Morristown, TN

Tena's Holiday Rice

My family likes rice and I cook it often. Whenever I do, I make a large quantity and refrigerate the extra. This recipe using leftover rice is easy to prepare. The olives give it a special flavor.

Makes 6 to 8 servings

1/4 c. butter
2 c. cooked rice
1/2 c. fresh or canned tomato, diced
1/4 c. celery, chopped
1/3 c. onion, chopped
1/4 c. chopped green olives with
   pimentos
1 T. fresh parsley, chopped
1 t. salt
1 t. pepper

Melt butter in a large non-stick skillet over medium heat. Add cooked rice; cook and stir until rice softens. Reduce heat to low. Add remaining ingredients and simmer for about 10 minutes.

Tena's Holiday Rice

Rosemarie Beron, Hockessin, DE

Zucchini Parmesan

This is a great side dish to use up all the zucchini from your garden. To make it a main dish, just add spaghetti! This dish reheats well in the oven and tastes even better a day later, after flavors have had a chance to blend.

Serves 6

1/2 c. all-purpose flour
salt and pepper to taste
2 small or 1 large zucchini, peeled
    and sliced 1-inch thick
2 eggs, beaten
1/4 c. grated Parmesan cheese
1/2 t garlic powder
Optional: small amount milk
1 c. dry bread crumbs
1/2 c. olive oil, divided
32-oz. jar spaghetti sauce
8-oz. pkg. shredded mozzarella
    cheese

Combine flour, salt and pepper in a plastic zipping bag; shake to blend. Add zucchini slices, a few at a time, shaking bag to coat well; set aside. In a bowl, whisk together eggs, Parmesan cheese and garlic powder. If mixture is to thick, stir in a few drops of milk. Dip floured zucchini slices unto egg mixture, then into bread crumbs; coat well with bread crumbs. Heat 1/4 cup oil in a skillet. Add zucchini slices in a single layer; cook until crisp and golden on both sides. Drain on paper towels. Repeat, adding more oil as needed. Place slices on an aluminum foil-lined rimmed baking sheet. Top with spaghetti sauce and mozzarella cheese. Bake at 400 degrees for 5 to 10 minutes, until cheese is melted and golden. If desired, place under the broiler to melt the cheese faster.

Jo Ann, Gooseberry Patch

Saucy Limas

These are some of the best lima beans you'll ever taste! They've got a tangy kick that will have you coming back for more.

Serves 6

2 10-oz. pkgs. frozen baby
    lima beans
1/2 c. catsup
1/4 c. molasses
1 T. mustard
1 T. vinegar
1/8 t. Worcestershire sauce
1/8 t. hot pepper sauce

Cook lima beans in a cast-iron skillet according to package directions. Drain; stir in remaining ingredients. Simmer over medium-low heat for 5 to 10 minutes, stirring occasionally, until heated through.

Saucy Limas

Kathy Courington, Canton, GA

Dilled Peas & Mushrooms

My husband is not fond of peas, but he likes this easy side dish. It seems like a special dish because of the mushrooms and chopped pimentos.

Makes 4 to 6 servings

1/2 c. onion, finely chopped
2 c. frozen peas, thawed
4-oz. can sliced mushrooms
1/2 t. dried dill weed
Optional: 2-oz. jar chopped pimentos

In a skillet sprayed with non-stick vegetable spray, sauté onion over medium heat for 5 minutes. Add peas, mushrooms with liquid, dill weed and pimentos with liquid, if using. Mix well and cover. Reduce heat to low. Simmer for 5 minutes, or until heated through.

Nancie Flynn, Bear Creek Township, PA

Gram's Zucchini in a Pan

This one-pan side dish is easy to make and uses up lots of our produce from our summer garden. We like to try different types of cheeses sometimes, just for variety.

Makes 6 servings

1/4 c. olive oil
1 onion, thinly sliced and separated
   into rings
4 to 5 sweet Italian peppers, sliced
2 zucchini, thinly sliced
2 tomatoes, diced
1 t. Italian seasoning
salt and pepper to taste
3/4 c. shredded Cheddar cheese

Heat olive oil in a skillet over medium heat. Add onion and peppers; cover and cook until soft, about 5 minutes. Stir in zucchini, tomatoes and seasonings. Cover and cook to desired tenderness. Remove from heat; stir in cheese. Cover and let stand until cheese melts; serve warm.

Gram's Zucchini in a Pan

Sonia Hawkins, Amarillo, TX

Roasted Okra Fries

I love okra cooked this way and it is healthier than fried okra! We use this recipe to roast cauliflower, broccoli, zucchini, yellow squash and Brussels sprouts. Asparagus too...sprinkle with 1/4 cup grated Parmesan cheese the last 5 minutes of roasting. Yum!

Serves 4

1 lb. fresh okra
2 T. olive oil
1/4 t. garlic powder
salt and pepper to taste

Rinse okra and pat dry with a paper towel. Trim off stem ends; cut okra into slices and place in a large bowl. Drizzle with olive oil and toss to coat well. Sprinkle with seasonings. Spread okra on a greased sheet pan. Bake at 425 degrees for 20 minutes, or until okra is crisp and golden.

Bev Fisher, Mesa, AZ

Tomato Salad with Grilled Bread

I found this unusual recipe and then tweaked it to make it my own. It's great for backyard barbecues. I guarantee you'll like it, too!

Serves 6

4 lbs. tomatoes, cut into chunks
2 cucumbers, peeled and sliced
4-oz. container crumbled reduced-
    fat feta cheese
1/4 c balsamic vinegar
1/4 t. pepper
4 thick slices crusty whole-grain
    bread, cubed
1 c. watermelon, cut into 1/2-inch
    cubes
1 red onion, very thinly sliced and
    separated into rings
2 T. sliced black olives, drained
1 T. canola oil
1/4 c. fresh basil, torn

Combine tomatoes, cucumber, cheese, vinegar and pepper in a large serving bowl. Toss to mix; cover and chill one hour. Place bread cubes on an ungreased baking sheet. Bake at 350 degrees for 5 minutes, or until lightly golden. At serving time, add bread cubes and remaining ingredients to tomato mixture. Toss very lightly and serve immediately.

Tomato Salad with Grilled Bread

Linda Hendrix, Moundville, MO

Golden Parmesan Roasted Potatoes

Pop into the oven alongside a roast for a homestyle dinner that can't be beat.

Serves 4 to 6

1/4 c. all-purpose flour
1/4 c. grated Parmesan cheese
3/4 t. salt
1/8 t. pepper
6 potatoes, peeled and cut
   into wedges
1/3 c. butter, melted
Garnish: fresh parsley, chopped

Place flour, cheese, salt and pepper in a large plastic zipping bag; mix well. Add potato wedges; shake to coat. Pour butter into a baking sheet pan, tilting to coat; arrange potatoes in pan. Bake, uncovered, at 375 degrees for one hour. Sprinkle with parsley.

Kelley Nicholson, Gooseberry Patch

Arugula Potato Cornugula

A fast and easy recipe. Let your kids help you toss in the ingredients one by one, and with each ingredient come up with a silly word that rhymes with arugula. They're sure to give this side dish a try!

Makes 4 servings

2 T. butter
1 t. garlic, minced
6 new redskin potatoes, sliced
1/4 t. salt
1/4 t. pepper
1 c. frozen corn
1/2 c. frozen lima beans
1 c. fresh arugula, torn
salt and pepper to taste

Melt butter in a large skillet over medium heat; cook garlic until tender. Stir in potatoes and seasoning. Cover and cook until tender, about 10 minutes, turning occasionally. Add corn and beans; cook until potatoes are tender, about 8 to 10 minutes. Season with salt and pepper. Add arugula; cover and let stand until arugula is wilted.

Arugula Potato Cornugula

Denise Piccirilli, Huber Heights, OH

Roasted Butternut Squash

This simple recipe is one of our all-time favorite sides. I know you will like it too!

Makes 4 servings

4 c. butternut squash, halved and
    seeds removed
2 T. extra-virgin olive oil
1 T. fresh rosemary, snipped
2 t. kosher salt
1 t. pepper

Dice butternut squash and spread on an ungreased baking sheet. Drizzle with olive oil; add seasonings and toss with your hands. Bake, uncovered, at 400 degrees for 30 to 40 minutes, until tender and golden, stirring once. Season with additional salt and pepper, if desired.

Janie Reed, Dresden, OH

Fried Green Tomatoes

Heat up your skillet to make this hot, buttery favorite. Tomatoes never tasted better...yum!

Serves 4

1-1/2 to 2 c. cornmeal
salt, pepper and seasoning salt
    to taste
2 green tomatoes, sliced 1/4-inch
    thick
oil or shortening for frying

Combine cornmeal and seasonings in a large plastic zipping bag. Shake to mix well. Add tomato slices, and gently shake to coat. Remove tomatoes from bag, shaking off excess cornmeal mixture. Heat oil or shortening in a large skillet over medium heat; fry tomatoes until golden on both sides. Remove from skillet.

Brenda Wells, Summerville, SC

Skillet Squash Succotash

Need a new way to serve all that summer squash from the garden? Try this!

Makes 4 to 6 servings

1 T. butter
1 T. oil
4 yellow squash, thinly sliced
10-oz. can diced tomatoes with
    green chiles
11-oz. can corn, drained
1 t. garlic powder

Melt butter with oil in a cast-iron skillet over medium heat. Add squash and cook until golden, stirring occasionally. Stir in remaining ingredients. Reduce heat; cover and simmer for 20 minutes.

Skillet Squash Succotash

Jen Licon-Connor, Gooseberry Patch

Market-Fresh Carrots

A zippy side dish...ready in only 10 minutes! Yes, it is easy, but it is oh-so-good!

Serves 4

1 T. olive oil
3 c. baby carrots
1-1/2 T. balsamic vinegar
1 T. brown sugar, packed

Heat oil in a medium skillet over medium heat. Add carrots; sauté for 10 minutes, or until tender. Stir in vinegar and brown sugar; toss to coat.

Tina Wright, Atlanta, GA

Simple Skillet Peaches

These peaches are delicious on just about anything you can think of. Cereal, oatmeal, ice cream, cobbler... or use them to top big slices of angel food cake!

Makes about 6 servings

6 c. peaches, peeled, pitted and cut
   into bite-size pieces
1/2 c. sugar
1 T. vanilla extract

Combine peaches and sugar in a large skillet over medium heat. Bring to a boil; reduce heat to medium-low. Simmer until peaches are soft and mixture has thickened, about 20 to 25 minutes. Stir in vanilla. Serve warm or store in an airtight container in the refrigerator.

Wendy Sensing, Brentwood, TN

Green Bean Bundles

Easy and delicious! The most obvious time-saver in this recipe is to skip making the bundles, but it is definitely worth the effort.

Serves 8

3 14-1/2 oz. cans whole green
   beans, drained
8 slices bacon, cut in half crosswise
6 T. butter, melted
1/2 c. brown sugar, packed
2 to 3 cloves garlic, minced

Gather beans into bundles of 10; wrap each bundle with a half-slice of bacon. Arrange bundles in a lightly greased small sheet pan. Mix melted butter, brown sugar and garlic in a small bowl; spoon over bundles. Cover and bake at 375 degrees for 30 minutes. Uncover and bake 15 more minutes.

Green Bean Bundles

Brandi Joiner, Minot, ND

Pasta Puttanesca

Such a versatile recipe! It's good either warm or cold.

Serves 6

16-oz. pkg. rotini pasta, uncooked
1 red onion, chopped
1 T. olive oil
5-oz. jar sliced green olives with
    pimentos, drained
4-oz. can sliced black olives, drained
24-oz. jar marinara sauce
Garnish: grated Parmesan cheese

Cook pasta according to package directions; drain. Meanwhile, in a large skillet over medium heat, sauté onion in olive oil until soft. Add olives; continue to sauté for another 2 to 3 minutes. Add pasta to the skillet and toss to mix. Add marinara sauce; stir well and heat through. Garnish with Parmesan cheese.

Lisa Johnson, Hallsville, TX

Crispy Potato Fingers

My mama always made these "tater fingers" for my kids when they came for a visit. The kids are both grown now, but they still love it when Granny makes these yummy potatoes!

Serves 4

3 c. corn flake cereal
3 T. grated Parmesan cheese
1 T. paprika
1/4 t. garlic salt
1/4 c. butter, melted
2 potatoes, peeled and cut into strips

Place cereal, cheese and seasonings in a blender or food processor. Cover and blend until crushed and well mixed. Pour cereal mixture into a pie plate or shallow dish; place melted butter in a separate shallow dish. Dip potato strips in butter and then in cereal mixture, coating well. Arrange potato strips on a greased baking sheet. Bake at 375 degrees for 25 minutes, or until potatoes are tender and golden.

Crispy Potato Fingers

Lyuba Brooke, Jacksonville, FL

Roasted Tomato-Feta Broccoli

This is such a simple and fast side. Don't let the easiness of it fool you... this dish is full of flavor and it's really healthy.

Serves 2 to 4

2 T. olive oil
2 c. broccoli flowerets
1 c. cherry tomatoes
1 t. lemon juice
dried parsley, salt and pepper
　to taste
1/2 c. crumbled feta cheese
Optional: additional olive oil

Heat oil in a skillet over medium heat. Add broccoli, tomatoes, lemon juice and seasonings; cook until vegetables are crisp-tender. Transfer warm vegetable mixture to a large bowl and mix in cheese. Drizzle with additional olive oil, if desired.

Michelle Powell, Valley, AL

Comforting Creamed Corn

Fresh corn, cut right off the cob makes this dish unforgettable. But if the season is not right for fresh corn, frozen corn works very well too. No matter what corn you use, this recipe will be a family favorite!

Makes 8 servings

1 T. butter
4 c. corn, thawed if frozen
1/2 c. plain Greek yogurt
2 T. grated Parmesan cheese
1 t. dried basil

Melt butter in a non-stick skillet over medium heat; add corn. Cook for about 6 minutes, stirring occasionally, until tender. Reduce heat; stir in yogurt and cook for 4 minutes. Stir in cheese and basil just before serving.

Comforting Creamed Corn

Rachel Anderson, Livermore, CA

Granny's Country Cornbread

Pour the batter into vintage corn stick pans...the kids will love 'em!

Makes 4 to 6 servings

1-1/4 c. cornmeal
3/4 c. all-purpose flour
5 T. sugar
2 t. baking powder
1/2 t. salt
1 c. buttermilk
1/3 c. oil
1 egg, beaten
1 c. shredded sharp Cheddar cheese
1 c. corn
1 T. jalapeño pepper, minced

Mix together cornmeal, flour, sugar, baking powder and salt in a large bowl. Make a well in center; pour in buttermilk, oil and egg. Stir just until ingredients are lightly moistened. Fold in cheese, corn and jalapeño; pour into a greased 8" cast-iron skillet. Bake at 375 degrees for 20 minutes, or until a tester inserted in the center comes out clean. Let cool slightly; cut into wedges.

Stephanie Norton, Saginaw, TX

Company Green Beans

A simple way to jazz up green beans.

Serves 4

3 slices bacon
1/4 c. red onion, finely grated
2 t. garlic, minced
2 14-1/2 oz. cans French-style
   green beans, drained
1 tomato, chopped
salt and pepper to taste
1/2 c. shredded sharp Cheddar
   cheese

Cook bacon in a cast-iron skillet over medium-high heat until crisp. Remove bacon to paper towels, reserving drippings in skillet. Sauté onion and garlic in reserved drippings until slightly softened. Remove from heat; stir in green beans, tomato and seasonings. Sprinkle with cheese. Cover the skillet and transfer to oven. Bake at 400 degrees for 15 minutes. Uncover; reduce heat to 350 degrees. Bake an additional 15 minutes, until hot and bubbly.

Company Green Beans

Jody Sinkula, Dresser, WI

Honeyed Carrots

The sweet taste of these carrots makes this a very popular dish!

Makes 8 servings

5 c. carrots, peeled and sliced
1/4 c. honey
1/4 c. butter, melted
2 T. brown sugar, packed
2 T. fresh parsley, chopped
1/4 t. salt
1/8 t. pepper

Place carrots in a cast-iron skillet; add water to cover. Cook over medium heat just until tender; drain and return to skillet. Combine remaining ingredients in a small bowl and blend well. Pour honey mixture over carrots; toss to coat. Cook over medium heat until carrots are glazed and heated through.

Marcia Shaffer, Conneaut Lake, PA

Grandma's Skillet Tomatoes

This recipe is so easy and it's always a hit with the guys!

Serves 6

1/4 c. milk
1/2 c. seasoned dry bread crumbs
1 T. green onion, minced
1 T. grated Parmesan cheese
1 t. Italian seasoning
1 t. salt
6 ripe tomatoes, sliced 1/2-inch
    thick
1/4 c. olive oil, divided
1/2 c. shredded mozzarella cheese

Place milk in a shallow bowl. In a separate bowl, combine bread crumbs, green onion, Parmesan cheese and seasonings; mix well. Dip tomatoes into milk; coat with crumb mixture. Heat 2 tablespoons oil in a cast-iron skillet over medium-high heat. Cook tomatoes, a few at a time, until golden, about 2 minutes per side. Add more oil, as needed. Remove tomatoes to a serving plate; sprinkle with mozzarella cheese.

Grandma's Skillet Tomatoes

Julie Vidovich, Winston-Salem, NC

Garlicky Parmesan Asparagus

Savor the flavor of garden-fresh asparagus in this simple recipe... nice with a baked ham.

Makes 4 servings

1 T. butter
1/4 c. olive oil
2 cloves garlic, minced
1 lb. asparagus spears, trimmed
2 t. lemon juice
salt and pepper to taste
Garnish: shredded Parmesan cheese

Combine butter and oil in a skillet over medium heat. Add garlic and sauté for one to 2 minutes. Add asparagus and cook to desired tenderness, stirring occasionally, about 10 minutes. Drain; sprinkle asparagus with lemon juice, salt and pepper. Arrange on serving platter; sprinkle with Parmesan.

Carole Larkins, Elmendorf AFB, AK

Fettuccine with Asparagus

Fresh asparagus and dill pair up with creamy fettuccine for a refreshing springtime side dish.

Serves 4 to 6

8-oz. pkg. fettuccine, uncooked
1 lb. asparagus, cut into 1/2-inch pieces
1 c. whipping cream
2 T. fresh dill, chopped
1 T. prepared horseradish
Optional: 4 oz. smoked salmon, cut into 1/2-inch pieces
1/2 t. salt
1/4 t. pepper
freshly squeezed lemon juice

Cook pasta according to package directions; add asparagus during last 3 minutes of cooking time. Drain and set aside. Heat cream, dill and horseradish in a skillet over low heat about one minute or until hot; add pasta mixture, tossing to mix. Gently toss in salmon if using; add salt and pepper. Squeeze lemon juice over top.

Fettuccine with Asparagus

Vickie, Gooseberry Patch

Creamy Bacon & Herb Succotash

You'll love this deluxe version of an old harvest-time favorite...I do!

Serves 6

1/4 lb. bacon, chopped
1 onion, diced
10-oz. pkg. frozen lima beans
1/2 c. water
salt and pepper to taste
10-oz. pkg. frozen corn
1/2 c. whipping cream
1-1/2 t. fresh thyme, minced
Garnish: 2 t. fresh chives, snipped

Cook bacon until crisp in a large skillet over medium-high heat. Remove bacon, reserving about 2 tablespoons drippings in skillet. Add onion; sauté about 5 minutes, or until tender. Add beans, water, salt and pepper; bring to a boil. Reduce heat; cover and simmer about 5 minutes. Stir in corn, whipping cream and thyme; return to a simmer. Cook until vegetables are tender, about 5 minutes. Toss with bacon and chives.

Dana Harpster, Kansas City, MO

Green Peas with Crispy Bacon

Rather than chase little round peas around the plate, be sure to serve this side with homemade biscuits, or "pea pushers," to help you get every pea on your fork.

Serves 6

2 slices bacon
1 shallot, sliced
1/2 t. orange zest
1/2 c. fresh orange juice
1/2 t. pepper
1/4 t. salt
16-oz. pkg. frozen sweet green peas, thawed
1 t. butter
1 T. fresh mint, chopped
Garnish: fresh mint sprig

Cook bacon in a skillet over medium heat until crisp; remove and drain on paper towels, reserving one teaspoon drippings in skillet. Crumble bacon and set aside. Sauté shallot in hot bacon drippings over medium-high heat 2 minutes or until tender. Stir in orange zest, orange juice, pepper and salt. Cook, stirring occasionally, 5 minutes or until reduced by half. Add peas and cook 5 more minutes; stir in butter and chopped mint. Transfer peas to a serving dish and sprinkle with crumbled bacon. Garnish, if desired.

Green Peas with Crispy Bacon

Amber Erskine, Hartland, VT

Hot Bacon-Potato Salad

This salad is just right for toting to a family reunion.

Makes 4 to 6 servings

1/4 lb. bacon
3/4 c. celery, sliced
1/2 c. onion, chopped
1-1/2 T. all-purpose flour
3/4 c. water
1/3 c. vinegar
2 T. sugar
1-1/2 t. salt
1 t. mustard
1/4 t. celery seed
4 c. potatoes, peeled,
    cooked and sliced

Cook bacon in a skillet over medium heat until crisp. Remove bacon; crumble and set aside. Add celery and onion to drippings in skillet; cook until tender. Add remaining ingredients except potatoes; cook until thickened, stirring constantly. Fold in potatoes and bacon; heat through. Serve warm.

Kelly Gray, Weston, WV

Spicy Carrot French Fries

These French fries are such a beautiful color and so very good for you as well!

Makes 4 to 6 servings

2 lbs. carrots, peeled and cut into
    matchsticks
4 T. olive oil, divided
1 T. seasoned salt
2 t. ground cumin
1 t. chili powder
1 t. pepper
Garnish: ranch salad dressing

Place carrots in a plastic zipping bag. Sprinkle with 3 tablespoons oil and seasonings; toss to coat. Drizzle remaining oil over a sheet pan; place carrots in a single layer on sheet pan. Bake, uncovered, at 425 degrees for 25 to 35 minutes, until carrots are golden. Serve with salad dressing for dipping.

Spicy Carrot French Fries

Abby Snay, San Francisco, CA

Chicken Taco Salad

These little gems are jam-packed with yummy ingredients!

Makes 8 servings

8 6-inch flour tortillas
2 c. cooked chicken breast, shredded
1-1/4 oz. pkg. taco seasoning mix
3/4 c. water
2 c. lettuce, shredded
15-1/2 oz. can black beans, drained
    and rinsed
1-1/2 c. shredded Cheddar cheese
2 tomatoes, chopped
1/2 c. green onion, sliced
15-1/4 oz. can corn, drained
2-1/4 oz. can sliced black
    olives, drained
1 avocado, peeled, pitted and cubed
Garnish: sour cream, salsa

Microwave tortillas on high setting for one minute, or until softened. Press each tortilla into an ungreased muffin cup to form a bowl shape. Bake at 350 degrees for 10 minutes; cool. Combine chicken, taco seasoning and water in a skillet over medium heat. Cook, stirring frequently, until blended, about 5 minutes. Divide lettuce among tortilla bowls. Top with chicken and other ingredients, garnishing with a dollop of sour cream and salsa.

Melissa Hart, Middleville, MI

Zucchini Fritters

Here's a tasty way to get your family to eat their vegetables and use the surplus zucchini from your garden!

Serves 4

3-1/2 c. zucchini, grated
1 egg, beaten
2/3 c. shredded Cheddar cheese
2/3 c. round buttery crackers,
    crumbled
Optional: 1/2 t. seasoned salt
2 T. oil

Combine zucchini, egg, cheese, crackers and, if desired, salt in a large mixing bowl. If mixture seems wet, add extra crackers; shape mixture into patties. Heat oil in a skillet; fry patties about 3 minutes on each side or until golden.

Zucchini Fritters

Sweet Apple Tarts

CHAPTER FIVE

EASY & SWEET
Desserts

Chocolate Pinwheels, Page 220

Eva's Fruit Cobbler, Page 230

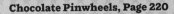

Gwendolyn Garren, Saluda, NC

Homemade Chocolate Cake

This is my favorite recipe for chocolate cake. It is very moist and the chocolate frosting is luscious.

Serves 15 to 20

1 c. butter
1/4 c. baking cocoa
1 c. water
2 c. all-purpose flour
1-1/2 c. brown sugar, packed
1 t. baking soda
1-1/2 t. cinnamon
1 t. salt
1/3 c. sweetened condensed milk
2 eggs, beaten
1 t. vanilla extract

In a small saucepan, melt butter over medium-low heat. Stir in cocoa and water. Bring to a boil; remove from heat. In a large bowl, combine flour, brown sugar, baking soda, cinnamon and cocoa mixture. Beat with an electric mixer on medium speed for 2 minutes, or until well blended. Beat in condensed milk, eggs and vanilla. Pour batter into a greased 15"x10" sheet pan. Bake at 350 degrees for 15 minutes. Spread Chocolate Frosting over warm cake.

Chocolate Frosting:
1/4 c. butter
1/4 c. baking cocoa
1 c. sweetened condensed milk
1 c. powdered sugar
1 c. chopped pecans

In a small saucepan, melt butter over medium-low heat. Stir in cocoa and condensed milk; remove from heat. Pour powdered sugar in a bowl; pour cocoa mixture over sugar. Beat with an electric mixer on medium speed until well combined. Stir in pecans.

Jean Burgon, Riverhead, NY

Apple Brownies

These apple bar cookies are just right for tucking into a lunchbox.

Makes one dozen

1/2 c. butter
1 c. sugar
1 egg, beaten
1 c. plus 1 T. all-purpose flour
1 t. cinnamon
1/2 t. baking soda
1/2 t. baking powder
1/4 t. salt
1 c. apple, peeled, cored and chopped
1 c. apple, sliced

Mix all ingredients together except sliced apple. Press into an ungreased 11"x17" sheet pan. Arrange sliced apples on top. Bake at 350 degrees for 40 minutes. Cool and cut into squares.

Apple Brownies

Charlene Sidwell, Altamont, IL

Frosted Cherry Drops

These have always been a favorite of our family. They're perfect for a colorful plate of cookies, either for home or as a gift.

Makes 2-1/2 to 3 dozen

18-1/2 oz. pkg. white cake mix
1/2 c. sour cream
1 egg, beaten
1/4 t. almond extract
3 T. maraschino cherry juice
1/2 c. maraschino cherries, finely
    chopped
Garnish: maraschino cherries,
    quartered

In a bowl, combine dry cake mix, sour cream, egg, extract and cherry juice; beat well. Fold in chopped cherries. Drop by teaspoonfuls onto ungreased baking sheets, 2 inches apart. Bake at 350 degrees for 8 to 12 minutes, until edges are lightly golden. Cool for one minute on baking sheets; remove to wire racks to cool completely. Frost with Cherry Frosting; top with quartered cherries.

Cherry Frosting:

2-1/2 c. powdered sugar
1/4 c. butter, softened
1 T. maraschino cherry juice
2 to 3 T. milk

Combine all ingredients in a bowl; stir until smooth.

Jodi Rhodes, Tolland, CT

Whole-Wheat Pumpkin Skillet Cake

This scrumptious recipe came out of the desire for a healthier cake. For a real show-stopper, top it with freshly whipped cream.

Makes 8 servings

1/4 c. butter, sliced
1/2 c. brown sugar, packed
1 egg, beaten
1/2 t. vanilla extract
1/2 ripe banana, mashed
1/3 c. canned pumpkin
1 c. whole-wheat flour
1/2 t. baking soda
1/4 t. salt
1/2 t. cinnamon
1/4 t. nutmeg
1/2 c. chopped walnuts
1/2 c. semi-sweet chocolate chips

Melt butter in a 9" cast-iron skillet over medium heat. Remove from heat; stir in brown sugar. Let cool. Whisk in egg; stir in vanilla. Add mashed banana and pumpkin; stir until blended and set aside. In a bowl, combine flour, baking soda, salt and spices. Add to pumpkin mixture in skillet; stir until well mixed. Stir in walnuts and chocolate chips; smooth top with spoon. Bake at 350 degrees for 15 to 20 minutes. Cut into wedges to serve.

Whole-Wheat Pumpkin Skillet Cake

Sherry Gordon, Arlington Heights, IL

Peanut Butter Surprise Cookies

Yum, yum, yum! I like to divvy up the dough between baking sheets and chill the second batch while the first is baking.

Makes one dozen

16-1/2 oz. tube refrigerated
    peanut butter cookie dough
12 mini peanut butter cups
1/3 c. semi-sweet chocolate chips
1 t. shortening

Divide cookie dough into 12 pieces. With floured fingers, wrap one piece of dough around each peanut butter cup. Place on ungreased baking sheets. Bake at 350 degrees for 10 to 15 minutes, until golden. Cool on baking sheets one minute; remove to wire rack to cool completely. In a saucepan, melt chocolate chips and shortening over low heat, stirring constantly. Drizzle melted chocolate over cookies. Let stand until set.

Jo Ann, Gooseberry Patch

Crunchy Biscotti

Afternoon or after dinner, you'll crave these treats with your next cup of coffee. I like to dress up these cookies with a drizzle of white chocolate!

Makes 3 dozen

3-1/3 c. all-purpose flour
2-1/2 t. baking powder
1/2 t. salt
1/4 c. oil
1-1/4 c. sugar
2 eggs, beaten
2 egg whites, beaten
Optional: melted white chocolate

Mix flour, baking powder and salt in a large bowl. In a separate bowl, whisk together remaining ingredients except optional chocolate. Blend flour mixture into egg mixture. Divide dough into 3 portions; knead each portion 5 to 6 times, and shape into a ball. Place dough balls on a parchment paper-lined 17"x 11" baking sheet. Shape into 9-inch logs; flatten slightly. Bake at 375 degrees for 25 minutes. Remove from oven; place logs on a cutting board. Using a serrated bread knife, cut 1/2-inch thick slices on a slight diagonal. Return slices to baking sheet, cut-side up. Bake for an additional 10 minutes at 375 degrees. Turn slices over; continue baking for 5 to 7 minutes. Let cool and drizzle with white chocolate, if desired; store in an airtight container.

Crunchy Biscotti

June Lemen, Nashua, NH

Frosted Sugar Cookies

We love to bake cut-out cookies for holidays year 'round...this recipe can't be beat!

Makes about 4 dozen

2 c. butter, softened
1-1/3 c. sugar
2 eggs, beaten
2 t. vanilla extract
5 c. all-purpose flour
Garnish: decorator sugars,
    candy sprinkles

Blend butter and sugar together; stir in eggs and vanilla. Add flour; mix until well blended. Shape dough into a ball; cover and chill for 4 hours to overnight. Roll out dough 1/4-inch thick on a lightly floured surface; cut with cookie cutters as desired. Arrange cookies on lightly greased baking sheets. Bake at 350 degrees for 8 to 10 minutes, until golden. Cool completely; frost with Powdered Sugar Frosting and decorate as desired.

Powdered Sugar Frosting:
4-1/2 c. powdered sugar
6 T. butter, melted
6 T. milk
2 T. vanilla extract
1 T. lemon juice

Combine all ingredients in a medium bowl. Beat with an electric mixer on low speed until smooth.

Brenda Derby, Northborough, MA

Apple-Cranberry Crisp

We like to make this using several different varieties of tart baking apples.

Serves 10 to 12

6 c. apples, peeled, cored and sliced
3 c. cranberries
1 c. sugar
2 t. cinnamon
1 to 2 t. lemon juice
3/4 c. butter, sliced and divided
1 c. all-purpose flour
1 c. brown sugar, packed
Garnish: vanilla ice cream

Toss together apple slices, cranberries, sugar and cinnamon. Spread in a greased skillet. Sprinkle with lemon juice and dot with 1/4 cup butter. Blend remaining butter with flour and brown sugar until crumbly; sprinkle over apple mixture. Bake for one hour at 350 degrees. Serve warm with vanilla ice cream.

Apple-Cranberry Crisp

Dianne Selep, Warren, OH

Coconut-Oatmeal Cookies

In the late 1960s, when my husband Ed was in the Navy, my mother and I would always send him care packages filled with cookies we had baked. Every time he received a package, everyone would crowd around and help him eat the cookies. These cookies were always the favorite.

Makes 5-1/2 dozen

2 c. all-purpose flour
1-1/2 c. sugar, divided
1 t. baking powder
1 t. baking soda
1/2 t. salt
1 c. brown sugar, packed
1 c. shortening
2 eggs, beaten
1/2 t. vanilla extract
1-1/2 c. quick-cooking oats,
    uncooked
1 c. chopped walnuts
1 c. shredded coconut

In a large bowl, mix together flour, one cup sugar, baking powder, baking soda and salt. Add brown sugar, shortening, eggs and vanilla; beat well. Stir in oats, walnuts and coconut; set aside. Place remaining sugar in a small bowl. Roll dough into walnut-size balls; dip tops in sugar. Place on ungreased baking sheets. Bake at 375 degrees for 12 to 14 minutes.

Janet Seabern, Winona, MN

Snowy Glazed Apple Squares

My mother used to make this dessert when I was a young girl. It is our family favorite!

Makes about 2 dozen

2-1/2 c. all-purpose flour
1/2 t. salt
1 c. shortening
2 eggs, separated
1/2 to 2/3 c. milk
1-1/2 c. corn flake cereal, crushed
8 baking apples, peeled, cored
    and sliced
1 c. sugar
1 t. cinnamon
2 T. powdered sugar

In a bowl, mix flour and salt; cut in shortening. Beat egg yolks in a measuring cup; add enough milk to measure 2/3 cup. Add to flour mixture and mix lightly. Divide dough into 2 parts, one slightly larger than the other. Roll out larger portion into a 15-inch by 10-inch rectangle. Place on a lightly greased 15"x10" sheet pan. Sprinkle evenly with cereal; arrange apple slices over cereal. Mix sugar and cinnamon; sprinkle over apples. Roll out remaining dough and place on top; seal edges and cut slits in top. Beat egg whites until foamy and spread over dough. Bake at 350 degrees for one hour. Cool slightly; sift powdered sugar over top. Cut into squares.

Snowy Glazed Apple Squares

Tina Knotts, Cable, OH

Snickerdoodles

I'll be sending care packages of this cookie to my daughter, Brittany, as she starts college this fall...it's her favorite!

Makes 3 to 4 dozen

1 c. butter, softened
1-1/2 c. plus 3 T. sugar, divided
2 eggs
2-3/4 c. all-purpose flour
2 t. cream of tartar
1 t. baking soda
1/2 t. salt
2 t. cinnamon

Blend together butter, 1-1/2 cups sugar and eggs; add flour, cream of tartar, baking soda and salt. Mix well; chill for one hour. Combine remaining sugar and cinnamon in a small bowl; set aside. Shape dough into balls; roll in sugar mixture. Arrange on ungreased baking sheets; bake at 400 degrees for 9 to 10 minutes. Let cool for 2 minutes before removing from baking sheets.

Mary Warren, Auburn, MI

Favorite Chocolate Chippers

The instant pudding in this cookie makes it extra chewy and good!

Makes 3 dozen

3/4 c. butter, softened
3/4 c. brown sugar, packed
1/2 c. sugar
2 eggs, beaten
1 t. vanilla extract
3.4-oz. pkg. instant vanilla
    pudding mix
2 c. all-purpose flour
1 c. quick-cooking oats, uncooked
1 t. baking soda
12-oz. pkg. semi-sweet chocolate
    chips
1/4 c. chopped pecans
Optional: pecan halves

In a large bowl, beat together butter and sugars. Beat in eggs and vanilla. Add dry pudding mix, flour, oats and baking soda; mix just until well blended. Fold in chocolate chips and nuts. Drop by tablespoonfuls onto greased baking sheets. Top each with a pecan half, if desired. Bake at 350 degrees for 12 to 14 minutes.

Favorite Chocolate Chippers

Chrissy Stanton, Odenton, MD

Toffee Almond Treats

So easy to make...so tasty to eat!

Makes about 2 dozen

1 sleeve saltine crackers
1 c. butter, melted
2 t. vanilla extract
1 c. sugar
12-oz. pkg. semi-sweet chocolate chips
1 c. sliced almonds

Line a baking sheet with aluminum foil; grease. Arrange crackers in a single layer on baking sheet; set aside. Stir together butter, vanilla and sugar in a saucepan; bring to a boil. Spread mixture over crackers; bake at 400 degrees for 4 to 5 minutes. Remove from heat; sprinkle with chocolate chips. Let stand until chips are melted; spread chips over sugar mixture. Sprinkle with almonds; chill for about 2 hours. Break into bite-size pieces.

Michelle Sheridan, Upper Arlington, OH

Chocolate Chip Tea Cookies

Make plenty of these sweet cookies!

Makes about 4 dozen

1 c. butter, softened
1/2 c. powdered sugar
1 t. vanilla extract
2 c. all-purpose flour
1-1/2 c. mini semi-sweet chocolate chips, divided

With an electric mixer on high speed, beat butter and powdered sugar until fluffy. Add vanilla; mix well. Gradually beat in flour; use a spoon to stir in one cup chocolate chips. Form into one-inch balls; place 2 inches apart on ungreased baking sheets. Bake at 350 degrees for 10 to 12 minutes. Remove to wire rack to cool. Place remaining chocolate chips in a small plastic zipping bag. Seal bag; microwave on high until melted, about 30 seconds. Snip off a small corner of bag; drizzle chocolate over cooled cookies. Chill for 5 minutes, or until chocolate is set.

Lisa Ashton, Aston, PA

Chocolate Pinwheels

This easy recipe uses refrigerated bread sticks for the dough...couldn't be easier!

Makes 16 pinwheels

11-oz. tube refrigerated bread sticks
3/4 c. semi-sweet chocolate chips
1/4 c. butter, melted
1/2 c. sugar

Unroll bread sticks and cut them in half. Press chocolate chips in a single row along top of each bread stick half; roll up into a pinwheel. Arrange pinwheels on a parchment paper-lined baking sheet. Brush with melted butter; sprinkle with sugar. Bake at 350 degrees for about 10 to 12 minutes, until golden.

Chocolate Pinwheels

Trysha Mapley-Barron, Wasilla, AK

Biscochitos Bars

In my early twenties, I moved to Santa Fe during the Christmas holidays. Biscochitos, the New Mexico state cookie, were everywhere. And I fell in love. Scented with cinnamon and anise, buttery and crisp...they were a cookie lover's dream. I created this pat-in-the-pan recipe, which eliminated the rolling and cutting of the standard recipe. I hope you enjoy these as much as we do!

Makes 5 dozen

2 c. butter, room temperature
1 c. powdered sugar
1 t. vanilla extract
3-1/2 c. all-purpose flour
1/2 c. cornstarch
4 t. anise seed, crushed
1 T. white wine or orange juice
1/2 c. sugar
4 t. cinnamon

Combine butter and powdered sugar in a large bowl. Beat together with an electric mixer on medium speed until light and fluffy. Mix in vanilla. Beat in flour, cornstarch and anise seed, just until well combined. Do not overmix. Pat dough into an ungreased 15"x10" sheet pan. Pierce all over with a fork. In a small bowl, combine sugar and cinnamon; set aside. With a pastry brush, lightly brush dough with wine or orange juice. Immediately sprinkle cinnamon-sugar evenly over dough. Bake at 325 degrees for 40 minutes, or until edges are lightly golden and cookies are set. Cut into bars while still warm.

Lisa Ashton, Aston, PA

Cinnamon Gingersnaps

These spicy-sweet cookies are so nice for dipping into a cup of hot coffee or herbal tea.

Makes 4 dozen

3/4 c. butter, softened
1 c. brown sugar, packed
1 egg, beaten
1/4 c. molasses
2-1/4 c. all-purpose flour
2 t. baking soda
1/2 t. salt
2 t. cinnamon
1 t. ground ginger
1/2 to 1 c. sugar

Blend together butter and brown sugar in a large bowl. Stir in egg and molasses; set aside. In a separate bowl, combine flour, baking soda, salt and spices. Gradually add flour mixture to butter mixture; mix well. Roll dough into one-inch balls; roll in sugar. Arrange on ungreased baking sheets, 2 inches apart. Bake at 350 degrees for 10 to 12 minutes, until cookies are set and tops are cracked. Remove to wire racks; cool completely.

Cinnamon Gingersnaps

Mary Bettuchy, Saint Robert, MO

Apple Butter Thumbprints

These cookies remind me of fall in New England, where I grew up. I can almost feel the cool autumn breeze whenever I bake them.

Makes 2 dozen

1/2 c. butter, softened
3/4 c. brown sugar, packed
1 egg, beaten
1/2 t. vanilla extract
2 c. all-purpose flour
1/2 t. baking soda
1/2 t. cream of tartar
1/4 t. salt
1/2 c. apple butter
1/2 c. sugar

In a large bowl, stir together butter and brown sugar until well blended. Beat in egg; stir in vanilla and set aside. In a separate bowl, mix together flour, baking soda, cream of tartar and salt. Stir into butter mixture until well blended together. Place sugar in a small bowl; set aside. Scoop dough by rounded tablespoonfuls, shaping into balls. Roll balls in sugar, coating completely; place on parchment paper-lined baking sheets. Press your thumb into the center of each ball, creating an indentation. Spoon apple butter by teaspoonfuls into indentations; do not overfill. Bake at 350 degrees for 8 to 10 minutes, until just starting to set up but still soft. Cool on baking sheets for 5 minutes. Transfer cookies to wire racks and cool completely.

Terri Lock, Waverly, MO

Charlotte's Chocolate Sheet Cake

My mother-in-law is famous for this yummy cake in our family...all 22 grandchildren request it when we get together.

Makes 2 dozen

3/4 c. butter
1 c. water
1/4 c. baking cocoa
2 c. all-purpose flour
1 c. sugar
1 t. baking soda
1/8 t. salt
1/2 c. buttermilk
2 eggs, beaten
Optional: chocolate frosting

Place butter, water and cocoa in a saucepan. Cook over medium heat until butter melts; let cool. In a mixing bowl, combine flour, sugar, baking soda and salt; mix well. Add butter mixture, buttermilk and eggs to flour mixture; stir well. Spread in a greased 15"x10" sheet pan. Bake at 400 degrees for 20 minutes. Drizzle with chocolate frosting if desired.

Charlotte's Chocolate Sheet Cake

Nina Jones, Springfield, OH

Apple Crisp Cookies

This yummy recipe won the 2016 "Best Cookie in the County" prize for me at the Clark County Fair in Springfield, Ohio.

Makes 3 dozen

1 c. butter-flavored shortening
1 c. brown sugar, packed
2 t. vanilla extract
2-1/2 c. old-fashioned oats, uncooked
2-1/4 c. all-purpose flour
1/2 t. baking soda
1/2 t. salt
1/2 c. water
1 t. cinnamon
1/4 c. sugar
21-oz. can apple pie filling, finely
    chopped

Combine shortening, brown sugar and vanilla in a large bowl. Beat with an electric mixer on medium speed until well blended. In a separate bowl, combine oats, flour, baking soda and salt. Add oat mixture alternately with water to shortening mixture; stir until well blended. Combine cinnamon and sugar in a small bowl. Reserve one cup of dough for topping. Shape remaining dough into one-inch balls. Roll each ball in cinnamon-sugar; place on parchment paper-lined baking sheets, 2 inches apart. Flatten each ball with the bottom of a cup coated with cinnamon-sugar. Bake at 375 degrees for 6 minutes. Remove from oven; cool on baking sheets for 5 minutes. Top each cookie with a dollop of pie filling and a sprinkle of Crumb Topping. Bake another 5 minutes. Cool on baking sheets for 2 minutes; remove cookies to wire racks.

Crumb Topping:
1 c. reserved cookie dough
1/4 c. old-fashioned oats, uncooked
1/2 t. cinnamon
2 T. brown sugar, packed
1/2 c. finely chopped pecans

Mix reserved dough with remaining ingredients until a crumbly mixture forms.

Marilyn Rogers, Point Townsend, WA

Apricot Layer Bars

Stir in some chopped pecans for crunchiness.

Makes one to 1-1/2 dozen

1-3/4 c. quick-cooking oats,
    uncooked
1-3/4 c. all-purpose flour
1 c. brown sugar, packed
1 c. butter, softened
1/8 t. salt
12-oz. jar apricot preserves

Mix together oats, flour, brown sugar, butter and salt. Press half of mixture into a greased 11"x7" sheet pan. Spread preserves over the top; top with remaining oat mixture. Bake at 350 degrees for 35 minutes. Let cool; cut into squares.

Apricot Layer Bars

Kay Kingsley, Indianapolis, IN

Aunt Betty's Pecan Squares

My family always looked forward to our visits to see Aunt Betty and her family over the holidays. We were always happy to find Pecan Squares in her cookie jar. We have made them countless times...hard to stop eating them!

Makes 2 dozen

1 c. butter, softened
1 c. brown sugar, packed
1 egg, separated
2 c. all-purpose flour
1 c. chopped pecans
1/2 t. salt

In a large bowl, blend butter and brown sugar. Add egg yolk; beat until fluffy. Add remaining ingredients except egg white; mix well. With your hands, press dough onto a greased 15"x10" sheet pan, all the way to the edges. Brush with lightly beaten egg white. Bake at 350 degrees for 20 to 25 minutes. Cool slightly cut into squares.

Virginia Watson, Scranton, PA

Easiest-Ever Sugar Cookies

So easy to mix up, even the kids can help...and of course, they will want to!

Makes 2 to 3 dozen

3.4-oz. pkg. instant vanilla
   pudding mix
1/2 c. sugar
1/2 c. butter
1 egg, beaten
1-1/2 c. all-purpose flour
1 t. baking powder
Optional: sanding sugar,
   candy sprinkles

Blend together dry pudding mix, sugar and butter; stir in egg and set aside. In a separate bowl, combine flour and baking powder; blend thoroughly into pudding mixture. Cover and chill until firm. Roll out dough 1/8-inch to 1/4-inch thick on a lightly floured surface; cut with desired cookie cutters. Place on lightly greased baking sheets. Bake at 350 degrees for 8 to 9 minutes. When cool, frost and decorate as desired.

Powdered Sugar Icing:
3 c. powdered sugar
2 to 3 T. milk
1 t. vanilla extract
few drops food coloring

Combine all ingredients in a large bowl. Divide icing into small bowls. Tint portions with food coloring as desired.

Easiest-Ever Sugar Cookies

Carol Brownridge, Ontario, Canada

Ginger Drops

The very first time I tried baking cookies, I was a bit nervous. I didn't have any experience baking and wanted to start with something easy, yet still delicious. A friend gave me this recipe knowing that I wouldn't fail as long as I followed these instructions.

Makes 2 dozen

4-1/2 c. all-purpose flour
2 t. baking soda
4 t. ground ginger
1-1/2 t. cinnamon
1 t. ground cloves
1/4 t. salt
1-1/2 c. butter
2 c. sugar
2 eggs, beaten
1/2 c. molasses
3/4 c. coarse sugar

In a bowl, stir together flour, baking soda, spices and salt; set aside. In a separate bowl, beat butter with an electric mixer on low speed to soften. Slowly add sugar, beating until combined; beat in eggs and molasses. Beat in as much of flour mixture with mixer as possible. Stir in any remaining flour mixture with a wooden spoon. Using an ice cream scoop, shape dough into 1-1/2 inch balls. Roll balls in coarse sugar. Place balls on ungreased baking sheets, 2 inches apart. Bake at 350 degrees for 12 to 14 minutes; for chewy cookies, do not overbake. Transfer cookies to a wire rack to cool.

Shelley Turner, Boise, ID

Eva's Fruit Cobbler

The combination of rhubarb and strawberries is a classic and oh-so-yummy in this dessert.

Makes 8 servings

4 c. rhubarb, sliced
4 c. strawberries, hulled and halved
1 c. sugar, divided
1/4 c. water
2 T. apple juice
1 T. cornstarch
1 c. all-purpose flour
1 t. baking powder
1/4 t. baking soda
1/4 t. salt
1/4 c. butter
1/2 c. buttermilk
1/2 t. almond extract
Garnish: 2 t. coarse sugar

In a large, oven-safe skillet, combine fruit, 3/4 cup sugar and water; bring to a boil. Reduce heat, cover and simmer for 10 minutes. Combine apple juice and cornstarch in a container with a tight-fitting lid; shake well to blend. Stir into fruit and cook until mixture thickens. Keep warm. Combine remaining dry ingredients, including remaining sugar, in a bowl. Cut in butter with a pastry blender or 2 forks until mixture resembles crumbs. Stir together buttermilk and extract; add to dough. Stir to blend well and drop by tablespoonfuls onto hot fruit. Sprinkle with coarse sugar. Bake at 400 degrees for 20 minutes, or until golden.

Eva's Fruit Cobbler

Diana Krol, Hutchinson KS

Oatmeal Scotchie Bars

These bars are quick, delicious and easy to bake. They are especially good with a tall glass of milk or a hot cup of tea.

Makes 3 to 4 dozen

1 c. butter, softened
1-1/2 c. brown sugar, packed
2 eggs, beaten
1 T. water
2 c. all-purpose flour
2 t. baking powder
1 t. baking soda
1 t. salt
1-1/2 c. quick-cooking oats, uncooked
1 c. butterscotch chips

In a large bowl, blend together butter and brown sugar until light and fluffy. Beat in eggs and water; set aside. In a separate bowl, combine flour, baking powder, baking soda and salt; mix well. Gradually stir flour mixture into butter mixture; blend well. Stir in oats, mixing well. Fold in chips. Spread batter in a greased 17"x11" sheet pan. Bake at 350 degrees for 20 to 25 minutes, until bars are lightly golden; don't overbake. Cool completely; cut into bars.

Lynda Robson, Boston, MA

Gingerbread Babies

Tuck them into a little box and leave them on someone's doorstep...surely you know someone who will give them a good home at Christmas or any time of year!

Makes about 12 dozen

3/4 c. butter, softened
3/4 c. brown sugar, packed
1 egg, beaten
1/2 c. dark molasses
2-2/3 c. all-purpose flour
2 t. ground ginger
1/2 t. ground allspice
1/2 t. nutmeg
1/2 t. cinnamon
1/4 t. salt

In a large bowl, blend together butter and brown sugar until fluffy. Add egg and molasses. In a separate bowl, combine remaining ingredients; gradually stir into butter mixture. Turn dough out onto a well-floured surface; roll out to 1/8-inch thickness. Cut dough with a 2-inch gingerbread boy cookie cutter. Place on greased baking sheets. Bake at 350 degrees for 9 to 10 minutes, until firm.

Gingerbread Babies

Laura Witham, Anchorage, AK

Perfect Pumpkin Purée

I love making my autumn dishes that include pumpkin purée. From pumpkin soup to pumpkin pie and everything in between, pumpkin purée is ever-present in my house during the autumn and winter months. This is something fun to do with your kids or even your sweetie on those blustery days and it makes your house smell so festive! Use a pie pumpkin...they have a naturally high sugar content and will taste the best.

2 to 5-lb. pie pumpkin

Cut off top of pumpkin and discard. Cut pumpkin into quarters; remove all the seeds and fibers. Cover a baking sheet with aluminum foil; spray with non-stick vegetable spray. Place pumpkin pieces pulp-side down on baking sheet. Bake at 375 degrees for one to 1-1/2 hours, until pulp is very soft. Once pulp is cooled, remove pulp from skin and either mash well or press through a potato ricer. Put pulp in cheesecloth and squeeze out any excess water. Pack pulp in plastic zipping freezer bags. If desired, premeasure and label for specific recipes. Keep frozen up to one year. Yield will depend on size of pumpkin.

Myra Mitten, Goldfield, IA

Grandma Mitten's Oatmeal Cookies

These oatmeal cookies are full of flavor and disappear quickly!

Makes 3 dozen

1 c. butter, softened
1 c. sugar
2 eggs, beaten
1 t. soda
2 T. hot water
2 c. flour
2-1/2 c. rolled oats, uncooked
1/2 t. salt
1 t. cinnamon
1/2 t. cloves
1 c. raisins
Optional: 1/4 c. chopped walnuts

In a bowl, blend butter and sugar until fluffy. Add eggs and mix well. Dissolve baking soda in hot water. Add to butter mixture and mix well; set aside. In a separate large bowl, mix flour, oats, salt and spices. Add to butter mixture and mix well. Stir in raisins and nuts, if using. Drop by tablespoonfuls onto lightly greased or parchment paper-lined baking sheets. Bake at 350 degrees for about 8 to 10 minutes, until lightly golden.

Grandma Mitten's Oatmeal Cookies

Cindy Jamieson, Ontario, Canada

Apple Turnovers

My mom would often make these turnovers during the cooler fall days. I've made a few changes, to add wonderful warmth to them. They are spectacular served with a scoop of ice cream, a drizzle of caramel sauce and a sprinkle of toasted almonds.

Makes 8 servings

4 Nova Spy or Granny Smith apples,
   peeled, cored and chopped
1/3 c. brown sugar, packed
1/4 c. all-purpose flour
1/4 t. cinnamon
1/8 t. nutmeg
1/8 t. ground cloves
1/4 t. lemon zest
1/2 t. lemon juice
1/2 t. vanilla extract
2 9-inch pie crusts, unbaked
1/4 c. milk, divided
2 T. sugar, divided
Garnish: vanilla ice cream, caramel
   sauce, toasted sliced almonds

In a saucepan, combine apples, brown sugar, flour, spices, lemon zest, lemon juice and vanilla. Cook over medium-low heat, stirring occasionally, until mixture comes to a boil. Reduce heat to low; simmer until apples are just tender. Cool slightly. Meanwhile, roll out one pie crust on a floured surface, 1/8-inch thick. Cut out 4 dough circles, each 4 inches in diameter; repeat with remaining crust. Spoon 1/4 cup filling to one side of each dough circle. Wet edges with a bit of milk; fold remaining dough over filling, pressing to seal the seams. Cut several small slits in tops of turnovers. Brush turnovers with milk and lightly sprinkle with sugar. Place on ungreased baking sheets. Bake at 350 degrees for 10 to 20 minutes, until golden. Serve turnovers warm, garnished as desired.

Sharon Demers, Delores, CO

Coconut-Lime Macaroons

These little nuggets of coconut goodness just can't be beat! Our entire family loves them!

Makes 3 dozen

3 egg whites, beaten
3 c. sweetened flaked coconut
1/4 c. sugar
4 T. all-purpose flour
1/4 c. lime juice
1 to 2 T. lime zest
1/4 t. vanilla extract

In a large bowl, combine all ingredients; mix thoroughly. Form into one-inch balls and place 1/2-inch apart on lightly greased baking sheets. Bake at 350 degrees for 12 to 15 minutes, until edges are lightly golden.

Coconut-Lime Macaroons

Gail Putjenter, Norfolk, NE

Easy Lemon-Coconut Bars

Tart-sweet and easy as 1-2-3!

Makes about 1-1/2 dozen

18-1/4 oz. pkg. angel food cake mix
2/3 c. flaked coconut
14-1/2 oz. can lemon pie filling
Garnish: powdered sugar

In a medium bowl, mix dry cake mix, coconut and pie filling just until blended. Pour into an ungreased sheet pan. Bake at 350 degrees for 20 to 30 minutes or until center is firm. Sprinkle with powdered sugar; cut into squares.

Kathi Rostash, Nevada, OH

Peanut Butter Texas Sheet Cake

Attention, peanut butter lovers! This moist cake has peanut butter baked inside the cake and mixed into the icing...plus a sprinkling of peanuts on top!

Serves 15 to 20

2 c. all-purpose flour
2 c. sugar
1/2 t. salt
1 t. baking soda
1 c. butter
1 c. water

1/4 c. creamy peanut butter
2 eggs, beaten
1 t. vanilla extract
1/2 c. buttermilk
Garnish: chopped peanuts

Combine flour, sugar, salt and baking soda in a large bowl; set aside. Combine butter, water and peanut butter in a saucepan over medium heat; bring to a boil. Add to flour mixture and mix well; set aside. Combine eggs, vanilla and buttermilk; add to the peanut butter mixture. Spread batter in a greased 15"x10" sheet pan. Bake at 350 degrees for 25 to 28 minutes, until cake springs back when gently touched. Spread Peanut Butter Icing over warm cake; sprinkle with peanuts.

Peanut Butter Icing:
1/2 c. butter
1/4 c. creamy peanut butter
1/3 c. plus 1 T. milk
16-oz. pkg. powdered sugar
1 t. vanilla extract

Combine butter, peanut butter and milk in a large saucepan over medium heat; bring to a boil. Remove from heat. Stir in powdered sugar and vanilla; stir to a spreading consistency.

Peanut Butter Texas Sheet Cake

Katie Majeske, Denver, PA

Caramel Apple Popcorn

Nothing says fall like apples and popcorn! You'll love this recipe!

Makes 8 to 10 servings

10 to 12 c. popped popcorn
2 c. dried apple chips, chopped
1/2 c. butter
1/2 c. light corn syrup
1 c. brown sugar, packed
1 t. vanilla extract
1/2 t. baking soda
Optional: 11-oz. pkg. caramel
   baking bits

Combine popcorn and apple chips in a large bowl; set aside. In a saucepan over medium heat, combine butter, corn syrup and brown sugar. Cook and stir until mixture boils. Boil without stirring for 5 minutes. Remove from heat. Add vanilla and baking soda; stir until foamy and light in color. Pour butter mixture over popcorn mixture; stir well. Place popcorn mixture onto large greased sheet pan. Bake at 250 degrees for 45 minutes, stirring every 15 minutes. Spread in a single layer on parchment paper-lined baking sheets to cool. If using caramel bits, melt as directed on package; drizzle over popcorn. Cool, then break apart. Store in an airtight container.

Kathleen Sturm, Corona, CA

Sweet Raspberry-Oat Bars

These layered bars with raspberry jam in the middle are my husband's favorite!

Makes 2-1/2 dozen

1/2 c. butter
1 c. brown sugar, packed
1-1/2 c. all-purpose flour
1/2 t. baking soda
1/2 t. salt
1-1/2 c. long-cooking oats, uncooked
1/4 c. water
2/3 c. seedless raspberry jam
1 t. lemon juice

In a large bowl, blend together butter and brown sugar until fluffy; set aside. Combine flour, baking soda and salt in a separate bowl. Stir flour mixture into butter mixture. Add oats and water; mix together until crumbly. Firmly pat half of oat mixture into the bottom of a greased 13"x9" sheet pan. In a small bowl, stir together jam and lemon juice; spread over oat mixture. Sprinkle remaining oat mixture over top. Bake at 350 degrees for 25 minutes. Cool completely before cutting into bars.

Sweet Raspberry-Oat Bars

Kelly Henkle, Vinton, IA

Crunchy Caramel Meltaways

My dad would make these goodies for me as an after-school treat...I couldn't wait to get home and enjoy one! Now I make them for my own children too.

Makes 2 dozen

6 c. corn flake cereal
14-oz. pkg. caramels, unwrapped
1/2 c. butter, sliced
1 c. milk
1/4 c. shredded coconut

Pour cereal into a large heatproof bowl; set aside. Combine caramels, butter and milk in a saucepan. Cook over medium-low heat, stirring constantly, until melted. Remove from heat; stir in coconut. Pour caramel mixture over cereal; stir until evenly coated. Drop by large spoonfuls onto wax paper-lined baking sheets; cool until set.

Kaela Oates, Waverly, WV

Pumpkin Bars

Similar to one of my favorite brownie recipes! Can't find pumpkin spice pudding? Use butterscotch for another yummy way.

Makes 16 to 20 bars

15-1/4 oz. pkg. yellow cake mix
3-1/2 oz. pkg. instant pumpkin spice pudding mix
2 c. milk
2 c. butterscotch chips

In a bowl, beat dry cake and pudding mixes with milk until thoroughly mixed. Pour batter into a greased 15"x10" sheet pan; sprinkle butterscotch chips on top. Bake at 350 degrees for 18 to 20 minutes. Cool; cut into bars.

Jill Ball, Highland, UT

Sweet Apple Tarts

I like to use Granny Smith apples in these tarts, but you can use any good baking apple that you like.

Serves 9

1 sheet frozen puff pastry, thawed
1/2 c. apricot jam
4 Granny Smith apples, peeled, cored and very thinly sliced
1/4 c. brown sugar, packed
1/2 t. cinnamon
1/2 c. pistachio nuts, chopped
Optional: vanilla ice cream

Roll pastry into a 12-inch square on a lightly floured surface. Cut pastry into nine 3-inch squares. Arrange squares on an ungreased baking sheet; pierce with a fork. Spoon jam evenly over each square; arrange apple slices over jam. Combine brown sugar and cinnamon in a small bowl; mix well. Sprinkle over apple slices. Bake at 400 degrees for 20 to 25 minutes, until pastry is golden and apples are crisp-tender. Sprinkle with nuts. Serve warm topped with scoops of ice cream, if desired.

Sweet Apple Tarts

Debbie Button, Jarrettsville, MD

Jenn's Pistachio-Cranberry Cookies

Last year my daughter Jenn and I were experimenting with some of our cookie recipes. She came up with this combination since the nuts, cranberries and chocolate chips were being used in other recipes. Voilà! Perfect for including in a cookie basket as an alternative to the traditional chocolate chip cookie.

Makes about 3 dozen

18-1/2 oz. pkg. yellow cake mix
2 eggs, beaten
1/2 c. oil
1/2 c. pistachio nuts, chopped
1/2 c. sweetened dried cranberries
1/2 c. white chocolate chips

In a large bowl, combine dry cake mix, eggs and oil; mix well. Fold in nuts, cranberries and white chocolate chips. Drop by teaspoonfuls onto ungreased baking sheets. Bake at 350 degrees for 12 minutes, or until edges are lightly golden. Transfer cookies to a wire rack to cool.

Carissa Ellerd, Thomaston, ME

Winslow Whoopie Pies

This delicious and often-requested family recipe is a huge hit at any social gathering.

Makes one dozen

1/3 c. baking cocoa
1 c. sugar
1 egg, beaten
1/3 c. shortening, melted and cooled
3/4 c. milk
2 c. all-purpose flour
1 t. baking soda
1/8 t. salt
1 t. vanilla extract
Optional: chocolate sprinkles

In a bowl, combine cocoa and sugar. In another bowl, beat egg and shortening. Add egg mixture to cocoa mixture; stir in remaining ingredients except sprinkles. Drop dough by rounded tablespoonfuls onto lightly greased baking sheets. Bake at 350 degrees for 15 minutes. Let cool on wire racks. Spread the flat sides of half the cookies with Marshmallow Filling; top with remaining cookies. Roll edges in sprinkles, if using.

Marshmallow Filling:
2 c. powdered sugar
2/3 c. shortening
2 T. milk
1/3 c. plus 1 T. marshmallow creme
1 t. vanilla extract

Combine all ingredients in a large bowl; stir until smooth.

Winslow Whoopie Pies

Jodi Eisenhooth, McVeytown, PA

Pecan Cookie Balls

Sweet, crisp little morsels to go with an after-dinner cup of tea or coffee.

Makes 2-1/2 to 3 dozen

1 c. butter, softened
4 T. powdered sugar
2 c. chopped pecans
1 T. vanilla extract
2 c. all-purpose flour
1 to 2 c. powdered sugar

Blend together butter and powdered sugar; add pecans, vanilla and flour. Wrap dough in plastic wrap; chill for about 3 hours. Form dough into 3/4-inch balls; place on ungreased baking sheets. Bake at 350 degrees for 10 minutes. Let cool; roll cookies in powdered sugar.

Eileen Blass, Catawissa, PA

Peanut Butter-Chocolate Bars

Top with marshmallow creme for s'more fun!

Makes 2-1/2 dozen

1 c. creamy peanut butter
1/2 c. butter, melted
1 c. graham cracker crumbs
16-oz. pkg. powdered sugar
2 c. semi-sweet chocolate chips,
  melted

Combine first 4 ingredients together in a large mixing bowl; mix well using a wooden spoon. Press into the bottom of a well-greased 15"x10" sheet pan; pour melted chocolate evenly over crust. Refrigerate for 15 minutes; score into bars but leave in pan. Refrigerate until firm; slice completely through scores and serve cold.

Vicki Nelson, Puyallup, WA

Zucchini Brownies

My mother gave me this recipe years ago after I married and started growing a garden. Like everyone else, I was always looking for ways to use up zucchini.

Makes about 1-1/2 dozen

2 c. all-purpose flour
1 t. salt
1/3 c. baking cocoa
1-1/2 t. baking soda
1-1/4 c. sugar
1/2 c. oil
1 egg, beaten
2 c. zucchini, grated
Garnish: chocolate frosting or
  powdered sugar

In a bowl, stir together flour, salt, cocoa and baking soda. Mix in sugar, oil, egg and zucchini. Spread into a lightly greased 15"x10" sheet pan. Bake at 350 degrees for 20 minutes. Let cool; garnish as desired.

Zucchini Brownies

Sue Ellen Morrison, Blue Springs, MO

Spirited Raisin Cookies

These cookies smell wonderful while baking...the taste is out of this world! My mother kept these on hand as an after-school treat.

Makes about one dozen

1/2 c. water
3 T. rum extract
1 c. raisins
1 c. butter, softened
1/2 c. powdered sugar
2 c. all-purpose flour
1/4 t. baking powder
1/4 t. salt

In a small saucepan over low heat, combine water, extract and raisins. Bring to a boil; remove from heat. Cover and let stand 30 minutes; drain. In a large bowl, blend butter and powdered sugar; set aside. In a separate bowl, mix flour, baking powder and salt; gradually stir into butter mixture. Fold in raisins. Roll out dough on a floured surface to 1/2-inch thick. Cut with cookie cutters, as desired. Place cookies on ungreased baking sheets. Bake at 375 degrees for 20 minutes. Cool on a wire rack.

Rhonda Reeder, Ellicott City, MD

Mix-and-Go Chocolate Cookies

When time is short, you'll appreciate this quick & easy recipe that everyone always loves!

Makes about 2 dozen

18-1/2 oz. pkg. chocolate cake mix
1/2 c. butter, softened
2 eggs, beaten
1 c. white chocolate chips

In a bowl, combine dry cake mix, butter and eggs; mix well until smooth. Mix in chocolate chips. Drop by tablespoonfuls onto ungreased baking sheets. Bake at 350 degrees for 8 to 10 minutes. Let cool on baking sheet for 5 minutes; remove to wire rack to cool completely.

Mix-and-Go Chocolate Cookies

Leona Krivda, Belle Vernon, PA

Frosted Pumpkin-Walnut Cookies

My family really likes these cookies! They're also a must on my Christmas cookie list.

Makes 7-1/2 dozen

1/2 c. margarine
1-1/2 c. brown sugar, packed
2 eggs
1 c. pumpkin
1/2 t. lemon extract
1/2 t. vanilla extract
2-1/2 c. all-purpose flour
1 T. baking powder
1/2 t. salt
2 t. pumpkin pie spice
1 c. chopped walnuts

In a large bowl, beat margarine with an electric mixer on low speed. Slowly add brown sugar; beat well on medium speed. Add eggs, one at a time, beating after each. Add pumpkin and extracts; beat until well mixed and set aside. In a separate bowl, mix flour, baking powder, salt and spice; slowly beat into margarine mixture until well blended. Stir in nuts. Drop by teaspoonfuls onto greased baking sheets, 2 inches apart. Bake at 375 degrees for 12 minutes. Cool on a wire rack; frost with Maple Frosting.

Maple Frosting:
1/4 c. butter
2-1/4 c. powdered sugar, divided
2 T. milk
3/4 t. maple flavoring

Beat butter with an electric mixer on low speed. Slowly add one cup powdered sugar; mix well. Add milk, flavoring and remaining powdered sugar. Beat well until smooth and creamy.

Vickie, Gooseberry Patch

Orange-Filled Napoleons

This dessert looks so fancy but it is so easy to make!

Makes 4 servings

8-oz. pkg. frozen puff pastry sheets, thawed
2 c. vanilla ice cream, softened
1 orange, peeled and thinly sliced
Garnish: powdered

Unfold pastry sheets and cut into 8 rectangles. Place on an ungreased baking sheet and bake at 375 degrees for 20 minutes, or until puffed and golden. Let cool. To serve, split pastries lengthwise. Spoon ice cream on one half; top evenly with orange slices and replace pastry top. Dust with powdered sugar.

Orange-Filled Napoleons

Index

Desserts

Mains-Vegetarian

Salads & Sides

Our Story

Back in 1984, our families were neighbors in little Delaware, Ohio. With small children, we wanted to do what we loved and stay home with the kids too. We had always shared a love of home cooking and so, **Gooseberry Patch** was born.

   Almost immediately, we found a connection with our customers and it wasn't long before these friends started sharing recipes. Since then we've enjoyed publishing hundreds of cookbooks with your tried & true recipes. We know we couldn't have done it without our

 friends all across the country and we look forward to continuing to build a community with you. Welcome to the **Gooseberry Patch** family!

Jo Ann & Vickie